"AN INDISPENSABLE AID TO ANYONE LOOKING FOR HELP FOR AN AGING RELATIVE."

—from the introduction by
Frederick R. Mugler, Jr., M.D.

It is one of the most difficult and most important decisions you and your family will ever have to make: how to provide the best possible supervision and health care, as well as the most comfortable and attractive surroundings, for an aging relative. But today, older Americans have more—and better—choices for their future than ever before.

Ted Rossi gives you an in-depth guide to all the medical, financial, legal, and emotional issues you will face. He helps you design a sensible plan of action, ease the transition into a nursing home, monitor the care your relative receives, and dramatically enhance the quality of life of everyone involved.

STEP
BY
STEP

helps you take special care of the very special people in your life.

STEP
BY
STEP

How to Actively Ensure the Best Possible Care for Your Aging Relative

TED ROSSI

WARNER BOOKS

A Warner Communications Company

Warner Books, Inc., 666 Fifth Avenue, New York, NY 10103

A Warner Communications Company

Printed in the United States of America
First Printing: May 1987
10 9 8 7 6 5 4 3 2 1

Library of Congress Cataloging-in-Publication Data

Rossi, Ted.
  Step by step.

  Bibliography: p.
    1. Nursing homes—Admission.   2. Nursing home
care.   3. Consumer education.   I. Title.
  RA997.R58 1987   362.1'6   86-28155
  ISBN 0-446-38428-3 (pbk.) (U.S.A)
          0-446-38427-5 (pbk.) (Canada)

Designed by Giorgetta Bell McRee

*This book is dedicated to
nursing home residents
everywhere*

Acknowledgments

During the years I spent researching this book, I benefited greatly from the cooperation of many professionals in the field of aging. First, I wish to thank the agencies mentioned in this book for their cooperation and assistance. I am also grateful to the following geriatric specialists who generously shared their knowledge with me:

Dorothy M. Nyce, M.D., Ph.D.; the late George A. Wood, M.D.; Walter M. Bortz II, M.D.; Frederick R. Mugler, Jr., M.D.; Jurate J. Dargis, Ph.D.; Marilyn Thompson, R.N.; Charlane Brown, D.S.W.; Vivian Wood, Ph.D.; and William F. Benson, U.S. Senate Committee on Aging. Hugh F. Lennon, J.D., also deserves thanks for contributing his legal expertise.

I owe a special debt of gratitude to my wife, Helen, who showed unwavering support, and to the many nursing home residents and their families who shared their experiences and perceptions with me.

Finally, I wish to thank those who assisted me in the preparation of the manuscript: George H. Warfel, Diane Sipes, Carol

Dondrea, and Jayne Walker; Barbara Gartner and the late Barbara Wardle, who typed the manuscript with patience and skill; and especially Laurie Harper, my literary agent, and Philip Core, whose editorial assistance gave this book the final form I had envisioned.

Contents

Introduction

As a doctor in private practice and later as a hospital-based physician closely involved for years with the care of elderly patients, I realized a long time ago that there was a need for a book like Ted Rossi's *Step by Step*. At last it is here.

A major requirement for functioning properly in our complex society is getting enough information to fully understand the choices we face and to make wise decisions on them. Fortunately, when it comes to the area addressed in *Step by Step*—health care for the elderly—the reader will find everything required for decision making in one place. Mr. Rossi's book presents a cornucopia of information derived from his personal experiences and meticulous research. He has been able to clear away the confusion about older people's health care needs, in the process supplying the reader with a lucid and trustworthy guide to this field. The facts are all here in a style that is sympathetic, supportive and very much to the point.

Step by Step should be immediately helpful to the relative or advocate of any elderly patient starting to have trouble with the activities of daily living. The range of assistance the reader may need will of course vary widely, but advice for all levels of care can be found in this book.

Transitions for the aging person from independent living to some system of support can be hard on all concerned, certainly for the patient and family, but also for the providers of care. No better manual currently exists for handling the adjustments involved in such transitions than Mr. Rossi's book. I am as pleased with its sensitivity to these personal issues as I am with its comprehensiveness.

Chapter 3, "Selecting a Nursing Home," is a particularly good section, dealing as it does with the most difficult decision the reader must face. Nursing homes are complicated places, and this chapter gives a remarkably clear look at their organization and operation. The matters of care that require appraising, the weaknesses and strengths that should be checked, are listed completely, and then the important point is stressed that one must rely finally upon the attitude of the homes' bedside staff for a successful placement. This kind of information is vital when selecting a facility for a relative.

Step by Step should prove an indispensable aid to anyone looking for help for an aging relative. Because of its overall crispness and completeness, I suspect it will be used by health care professionals as well. In particular, those doctors, nurses and social workers not regularly active in this special field should find it a rich source of help.

In summary, I recommend it to all general readers who have the future of aging relatives to consider. I believe my colleagues in health care delivery will find it a useful reference, too.

Frederick R. Mugler, Jr., M.D.
Clinical Associate Professor of Medicine
Stanford University School of Medicine
Stanford, California

Foreword

This book began during the endless hours I paced the corridors of the nursing home where my mother spent the last years of her life. Like most people, I had refused to think seriously about the possibility that someone I loved would end her days in a nursing home. Even after the three years of her serious illness, during which my wife and I had struggled to care for her in our own home, we were still caught unprepared when we finally had to face the fact that she needed more care than we could provide. Feeling helpless, not knowing where to turn for guidance, we made the best decision we could under the circumstances.

During the four years I spent walking the halls of nursing homes as a concerned family member and as a volunteer, I interviewed health care professionals, residents and their families. I learned things that would have helped me make a better choice of health care for my mother, as well as many ways to ensure that the quality of her life and the care she received in the institution I had chosen was as good as it could possibly be. Some of this knowledge came too late to help my mother, but the experience made me resolve to continue my investigation of nursing homes, supplementing my personal observations and interviews with a survey of the professional literature.

Americans are probably the world's best-informed consumers of cars, computers, microwave ovens and other accessories of the good life. But when it comes to the choice of health care for the elderly, which can cost an individual family $15,000 or more a year and can make the difference between life and death for the elderly and infirm, most people feel utterly helpless—not because we know nothing, but because we are paralyzed by the little we know. While the exposés of nursing homes that have been appearing since the sixties have produced many positive changes in the field of health care for the elderly, it is the well-documented horror stories that have captured the headlines. Few laypeople are fully aware of the good news that today's older Americans have more and better choices of health care than ever before. Even fewer know how best to choose among them.

This book is written to guide families through every step of the process of finding the best possible care for their aging parent, spouse, other relative, or close friend; that is, from facing the fact that help is needed and evaluating the alternatives the community has to offer to providing effective support and vigilance after the decision has been made. The choice of care for your older relative is one of the most important and difficult decisions your family will ever have to make. Instead of succumbing to the paralyzing feelings of impotence and guilt that so often accompany the crisis of a relative's failing health, you can play an active role in ensuring that he or she will receive the best possible care throughout the last years of life. The chapters that follow will give you the information and methods that will enable you to serve as an effective, well-informed advocate of your relative's or friend's best interests through every stage of the process.

No matter how much or how little time you have, your first task will be to assess all the facts—medical, emotional, and financial—of your relative's situation (Chapter 1). Once you understand exactly what his or her needs and resources are, the next step is to investigate the supportive programs your community offers its elderly residents to see whether you can find a viable alternative to a nursing home (Chapter 2). If you determine that a nursing home is the only solution that will suffice, you will want to undertake a rigorous evaluation of the most attractive homes in the area to make certain you choose the best one possible (Chapter 3).

Many people feel that when they are finally forced to place their relative in a nursing home, they are turning over to strangers all power and responsibility for care in the future. In truth, the active support and intervention of the family always makes a crucial difference in the quality of a nursing home resident's life and the quality of care received. Chapter 4 will show you how you can help to make the older person's entrance into the nursing home as comfortable as possible. Chapter 5 will give you a wealth of specific suggestions for enriching the quality of life in the home. With the information and methods contained in Chapter 6, you will be able to monitor the care your relative receives.

I hope that families who make use of the information and guidelines in this book will emerge from their painful process with the satisfaction of knowing that they have done the best anyone could do for aging loved ones.

STEP
BY
STEP

1

Facing the Facts

"What will we do about Mother? She fell again today getting out of the shower. And she seems more forgetful every time I see her."

"But what *can* we do?"

"I hate to say it, but it may be time to start thinking about a nursing home."

"Are you crazy? I can't imagine Mother in one of those places. She'd raise the roof if we ever suggested it!"

"But what will we do if she gets worse?"

"I don't know. I can't stand to think about it. Let's wait a while and see what happens."

Conversations more or less like this one take place every day in countless American families because it is so terribly hard to think about the day when someone we love will no longer be able to live an independent life. All of us prefer to imagine our parents, spouses and friends enjoying active, productive lives in their own homes forever, miraculously escaping the ravages of old age. Yet we all see that the aging process brings physical or mental changes that gradually—or suddenly—remind us that this familiar way of life must one day come to an end.

Because planning for the changing needs of the elderly forces us to confront this heartrending reality, too often older people and their families try to ignore the signs that help may soon be needed, until a sudden crisis forces immediate action. Then decisions must be made hurriedly, and choices seem terribly limited. Everyone feels helpless and victimized, both the elderly invalid and the family members who bear the burden of responsibility.

Ideally, planning for the needs of the aged should be an ongoing family process that begins early, before health problems reach a crisis stage, and actively involves the older person and everyone concerned with her or his welfare. By planning ahead, older people and their families will have time to investigate and take full advantage of the various community programs that can make their lives easier and more pleasant. A leisurely planning process will allow family members to think through and discuss sensitively and realistically with the older person the various future possibilities, taking into consideration the needs, desires and resources of everyone concerned. It will lessen the terrible burden of guilt adult children face when, with no preparation, they are forced to assume the responsibility of deciding the fate of a suddenly incapacitated loved one.

Of course, families faced with an unforeseen accident or acute illness will not have the luxury of long-term planning. Whether you have a year or only a week to decide on a course of action, you will probably want to share the responsibility with other concerned family members. Time-consuming and emotionally wrenching as this can sometimes be, particularly in view of the fact that you are placing the well-being of your relative in the hands of strangers, it will lighten your own emotional burden and at the same time enhance everyone else's feeling of commitment to the plan of action that emerges. It is particularly important to give the older person as large a role in the decision-making process as he or she is capable of assuming. As long as older people are still alert, they should be spared the unnecessary humiliation of being treated as helpless objects of our concern. Rather, we must treat them as active participants in determining their own future.

Whether your aging relative is in a hospital bed or still managing well at home, you will probably feel reluctant to initiate a discussion about the present or future need for help. The sooner these talks begin, however, the better the result will be for everyone concerned. You are likely to find that your older relative has thought long and hard about the future and feels greatly relieved that these fears no longer have to be faced alone.

Major life changes are very stressful for anyone and particularly for elderly people who have been accustomed to the same predictable routine for many years. It may take many hours of gentle but persistent effort by various family members before your relative begins to face the need to join you in the search for a realistic solution. If your best efforts fail, you should not blame yourself, but you should consider seeking help from outside the family. The intervention of a clergyman or physician whom the older person knows and trusts can do wonders to facilitate communication. Another excellent source of help is your local family service agency, which will be able to direct you to a multigenerational counseling program or at least to a social worker who is experienced in dealing with problems of this kind. The first and most important goal of these discussions, whether they take place within the family or with the help of professionals, should be to persuade your relative to join with you in a shared effort to assemble all the facts and arrive at the best possible plan of action for his or her future.

THE MEDICAL FACTS

The first step in planning for the health care of an older person is a thorough, professional assessment of his or her condition and needs. The kind of professional evaluation you should seek depends in part upon the nature of the problems your relative is experiencing. If the situation that precipitates the need for help is a straightforward medical condition such as a severe fracture, a debilitating attack of pneumonia, or a crippling case of arthritis, the primary care physician or specialist who has been treating the patient should be your first source of information. If the primary problem seems to be mental rather than physical, and the primary care physician confirms this diagnosis, you should seek out a mental health professional to conduct an evaluation of your relative's mental and emotional condition. You should be aware, however, that the problems that debilitate the elderly can be extremely difficult to diagnose correctly, and relatively few general practitioners or mental health professionals have sufficient training and experience in the rapidly developing field of geriatric medicine to give accurate assessments of all the complex combinations of physical, mental and emotional symptoms older people often present.

Leon J. Epstein, M.D., in "Clinical Geropsychiatry," and other authors in *Topics in Aging and Long-Term Care,* edited by William Reichel (see Bibliography), deal with the problems of mental deterioration. They discuss how so many older people experience what can easily be labeled as progressive, irreversible "senility," or what physicians call "chronic organic brain syndrome." In fact, many elderly people diagnosed as irreversibly senile and consigned to nursing homes on the recommendation of their family physicians might be cured of these symptoms if their conditions were properly identified and treated. Among the elderly, even extreme apathy, forgetfulness, disorientation or lethargy are often symptoms of any one of a number of treatable physical or psychological conditions, from diabetes or nutritional deficiencies to depression over the loss of a beloved spouse or friend.

Among the major causes of these treatable symptoms of apparent senility are overmedication and adverse side effects or interactions caused by prescribed drugs. Many older people take far too many pills in quantities and combinations that can be very dangerous. Even with the most benign medications, the normal dosages specified by the Federal Food and Drug Administration, which are based on the metabolism of young adults, are far too strong for many elderly people. When older people take more than the prescribed doses in the hope that more is better, or obtain a number of different prescriptions from various doctors, or trade medications with their friends, the result can be a condition that seems to be irreversible senility but is simply an adverse drug reaction.

In response to an increasing demand for better health care for elderly Americans, the field of geriatric medicine has been expanding rapidly in recent years. By now, many communities have thorough geriatric screening programs that make available the combined expertise of a team of physicians and mental health professionals, all specially trained to identify the particular physical, mental and emotional problems of the elderly. University and teaching hospitals, Veterans' Administration hospitals and health maintenance organizations have been particularly active in developing these programs, but by now, many community hospitals also offer this service.

Especially if the cause of your relative's physical or mental problems is more uncertain than a specific episode of illness or injury, an evaluation by a geriatric screening program can prove to be the single most important step you can take to ensure the best care. Your local hospital, county medical association, or family service agency should be able to direct you to a geriatric screening program or at least to a geriatric specialist in your area.

Because it is crucially important for everyone who plays a role in making health care decisions to understand the older person's physical and mental problems as thoroughly as possible, you or another trusted family member should arrange to consult with the primary care physician or geriatric specialist who is conducting the evaluation, either at the time of the physical examination or at a separate meeting. This consultation should offer an important exchange of information. The knowledge an adult child or other relative or friend has of an older person's medical history, personal habits and physical and mental state can often prove to be an invaluable supplement to the physician's professional observations. The kinds of changes in an older person's mental or emotional state that can indicate an adverse drug reaction, for example, may go unnoticed by a physician, but family members will observe them immediately. If you suspect that some of your relative's symptoms are drug-induced, you can investigate his or her pill-taking habits more thoroughly than a physician can, and you can also question the doctor about the possible side effects of the various medications or combination of medications the older person is taking. Ideally, this kind of interchange of personal and professional knowledge should result in an accurate and thorough understanding of the older person's condition for both the physician and the family.

THE FACTS OF INDIVIDUAL PERSONALITY AND CAPABILITIES

An accurate medical assessment of the older person's physical condition is only one component, although a major one, of the constellation of factors that should go into determining when your relative needs help and what kind of care is needed. A physician can tell you the nature and severity of an illness or injury, but you and the rest of your family are in a better position than any professional to observe how well or poorly your older relative is coping with physical problems. Especially in cases of chronic illness or disability, family members are often the best judges of whether the older person has the physical and emotional capacity to manage the details of everyday life and, if not, how much help is required.

It is an error for physicians and hospital discharge planners who advise the families of older people whose health is failing, to assume that institutionalization as a matter of course is the easiest, most straightforward solution for most patients and their families. Because you and other family members know your older relative far more intimately than any of the professionals possibly could, your own sense of his or her personality, capabilities and preferences should play an important role in deciding what form of care is best if there are any choices to be made. She or he will undoubtedly have strong feelings and preferences that should be heard and respected. If the older person desperately wants to remain at home rather than enter a nursing home, this is an emotional fact that the family must take into account. If the medical facts allow for the possibility of remaining at home with supportive care, the individual's personality, desires and emotional capabilities should be primary considerations in determining whether a nursing home is the best choice.

It is the role of the family to keep in focus all the personal patterns and preferences that define the older person's individual responses to failing health. Would your mother thrive on the challenges of managing her own life after she is released from the hospital with a fractured hip, or would she prefer the security of nursing home care? These are the kinds of questions that relatives can often answer better than professionals can.

What family members must guard against, however, is letting their own feelings blind them to the best interests of their relative. The desire to protect frail older people from the possible risks of independent living can sometimes lead families to make decisions that deny relatives the freedom they need to make their lives worthwhile. On the other hand, fiercely independent older people can adamantly deny the need for supportive care far beyond the point where help is needed. In cases like these, family members must overcome their own natural desire to avoid confronting the problem and make their own assessments of how well the older person is functioning alone.

The family's role in determining the kind of care that will be best is an extremely sensitive one, requiring a delicate combination of empathy and objective judgment. The more you can share this responsibility with other concerned relatives and with the older person whose life is to be affected, the less burdensome it will seem.

THE FINANCIAL FACTS

Unfortunately, the medical and emotional needs of the older person are not the only factors most families need to take into account in deciding how best to care for their ailing relatives. Financial considerations must also play a major role in the health care choices of most American families. As of this writing, the average cost of nursing homes nationwide is $1200 a month. In many areas, of course, charges can be far higher; and the total cost of the services needed to maintain an elderly person living at home can be higher still. Because a long-term catastrophic illness can so quickly exhaust the assets of elderly people—even those who have been financially secure all their lives—all but the wealthiest families may have to worry sooner or later about how to pay the bills. To ensure the future well-being of their relative, every family should make thorough, well-informed financial planning an important part of their decision-making process from the beginning.

Planning for the present and future needs of an older person should begin with a careful review of all the financial resources that are available for this purpose. This investigation will generally encompass four broad categories:

- An inventory of the elderly person's annual income, including pension plans, veterans' benefits, Social Security, rental property, or other sources
- A survey of his or her total assets—savings accounts, investments, real estate holdings, automobiles, or other valuable personal property
- A review of all private insurance policies
- A careful investigation of present and possible future eligibility for government assistance programs.

This may also be the appropriate time to begin discussing the issue of what financial assistance, if any, can be expected from various family members now or in the future.

Ideally, of course, an older person's estate planning should begin many years before a medical crisis forces a frantic, last-minute scramble to assemble this kind of information. In too many American families, money is a taboo subject until a grave emergency forces the issue. Because it can be so difficult to assemble the necessary facts and documents once the elderly relative is incapacitated, adult children should make every effort to begin dealing with this subject before a crisis occurs. Establishing a younger family member as a joint tenant on a parent's savings and checking accounts, for example, will greatly facilitate financial transactions in the event that the older person suddenly becomes incapacitated, even temporarily. The execution of power of attorney for the older person is equally important for ensuring that financial affairs can be handled in an orderly way even if she or he becomes too ill to deal with them.

Medicare

For the great majority of older Americans, Medicare, the federal government's health insurance program for the elderly, is the major source of protection against the soaring costs of medical care.

Medicare's Hospital Insurance (Part A) helps to defray the costs of inpatient hospital care. Its optional Medical Insurance (Part B) pays most of the bills for doctors' services, physical and speech therapy, outpatient hospital services and other necessary medical costs.

Unfortunately, Medicare insurance provides only limited coverage for the kinds of care required by so many elderly people with long-term chronic illnesses or disabilities. A resident of a skilled nursing home is eligible for Medicare coverage only if hospitalized for three consecutive days within fourteen days of admission to the home. After entering a skilled nursing facility, Medicare will cover the costs for only one hundred days a year. During these one hundred days, the resident's medical condition is closely monitored by a committee of physicians who will approve payment under the Medicare program for only as long as they determine that skilled nursing care is required on a daily basis. The Medicare program offers no assistance to the many older people who need long-term custodial care but do not require the level of medical care a skilled nursing facility provides, and its payments for in-home nursing services are restricted to one hundred visits a year.

If a medical condition makes an older person eligible for Medicare benefits, it is crucially important for families to know that *the program will cover the needed services only if they are provided by institutions or agencies that are certified under its guidelines.* Payment is based on its own schedule of fees, which may be significantly lower than the rates charged by individual institutions or agencies. Because Medicare's regulations are so complex and subject to such frequent changes, you should ask both the older person's physician and any health care facility you are considering to help you determine precisely which services will be covered by Medicare and for how long.

A recently introduced plan worth investigating is Medigap. Medigap is insurance that is supplemental to Medicare. For example, if Medicare covers 80 percent of the expenses, Medigap may cover the remaining 20 percent.

Private Health Insurance Plans

Because Medicare falls far short of meeting all the health care needs of older Americans, many elderly people purchase additional private insurance policies to supplement their Medicare benefits. Especially in cases of long hospital stays, the co-payment required by Medicare can prove to be extremely expensive; this is one of the gaps that private health insurance can fill. Unfortunately, most private insurance coverage for catastrophic long-term illness stops at age sixty-five. Few private insurance plans offer extended coverage for nursing home care, although some offer a modest addition to Medicare's one hundred days, and few policies cover the costs of any home health care services beyond those provided by a registered nurse.

Medicaid

These days, many elderly people who have worked hard and saved all their lives for their retirement are forced to turn to Medicaid assistance after long-term medical bills have exhausted their financial resources. Medicaid provides a wide range of medical benefits for older people whose incomes are low enough to meet its eligibility requirements. Because Medicaid is a shared federal/state program, its requirements vary somewhat from state to state. Your local Medicaid office, however, can give you their current requirements. Some state programs also provide some assistance to the "medically indigent"—people whose income is slightly higher than the established ceilings but insufficient to meet their medical expenses.

Unlike Medicare, Medicaid covers the cost of long-term skilled nursing home care for an unlimited period of time, as long as the institution is certified under the program's guidelines. It can also reimburse the costs of in-home nursing and custodial services as well as many other kinds of medical services for the elderly.

The first step in seeking Medicaid assistance is to call your local department of welfare, health administration or social services. You will find the office that deals with Medicaid listed in your telephone book under government offices. After discussing the situation briefly with a clerk, you can then make an appointment to talk with a staff member who will determine whether the older person is eligible for Medicaid. Instead of dealing with all this bureaucratic red tape, which can be both frustrating and confusing, you may prefer to work with a social service agency that can assign a case worker to help you through the entire process of deciding what to do for your older relative or friend.

Family Responsibility

Until fairly recently, adult children were expected to assume financial responsibility for the nursing home care of their aging parents. For the past decade, however, Medicaid regulations have abolished this as a legal obligation and have determined eligibility for government assistance solely on the basis of the individual's assets. Many adult children, of course, still contribute voluntarily to their parents' care, even though they are no longer required by law to do so. Some families have chosen to take advantage of the present situation by transferring the assets of elderly parents to their children to ensure that their life's savings will not be consumed by the ever-increasing costs of prolonged illness. In response to this all-too-common practice, a 1982 federal law allows states to crack down on this kind of misrepresentation by requiring a long waiting period after the transfer of substantial assets before an older person may apply for Medicaid benefits. The soaring government-subsidized cost of nursing home care to American taxpayers has led the Reagan administration, as well as a number of state governments, to explore the possibility of requiring that children once again contribute to their parents' medical care. In fact, at least three states have implemented Relative-Responsible Medicaid Rules under waivers from the Office of Health Care Financing Administration. So be sure to check the status of these regulations in your state.

The issue of spousal responsibility is more complicated. A 1979 federal regulation established that when a married couple lives in separate residences, their assets can be determined separately after six months of living apart. Thus, a wife confined to a nursing home may be judged eligible for financial assistance while her husband still has considerable assets. Many states, however, have their own laws that require a spouse to take full responsibility for the medical bills of his or her mate for an indefinite period of time. Even when a couple begins with substantial savings, it is quite possible for the healthy spouse to become virtually bankrupt before Medicaid assumes the nursing home bills of the mate. Faced with this tragic situation, some elderly couples have been forced to file for divorce to avoid complete financial ruin.

Realistic financial planning must take into account this possibility that costly in-home or nursing home care could be required for many years, diminishing or exhausting the older person's financial resources. Other family members will have to ask themselves and each other, early and honestly, whether they are willing and able to contribute to meeting these costs and, if so, how much and for how long.

Even families who never dreamed that their parents might someday have to depend on Medicaid benefits may find themselves facing that necessity after several years of nursing home bills. Because many nursing homes do not accept payment from the Medicaid program, families who have not anticipated this possibility are often forced to find another home for their relative when funds are exhausted. Painful as they are, these possibilities should be taken into account from the beginning to ensure that a financial crisis will not force a traumatic disruption in the accustomed life of the elderly person.

THE FACT OF CHANGE

The later years of life, like the early ones, can often be a time of changes that continually challenge the resources of individuals and their family. Families making health care decisions for the elderly must take into account the fact that no one can predict the future with absolute certainty. The most brilliant physician cannot tell you in advance exactly how quickly or how well an older person will recover from a serious injury or illness or how long anyone will suffer a terminal illness.

Everyone concerned with making health care decisions for older people should be aware that the immediate solution is not necessarily the final one. An elderly woman who breaks her hip or suffers a severe attack of pneumonia may need to be discharged from the hospital into a nursing home, but she may be able to return to her own home if her condition improves. On the other hand, the supplementary in-home services that allow an infirm older person to live independently for a period of time may no longer suffice once the disability becomes more severe.

Planning for the health care needs of the elderly is more often an ongoing process than a one time decision. The most responsible long-term planning should be flexible enough to anticipate all the future possibilities, so that families will be prepared to respond sensitively and quickly to the changing needs of their aging relative.

2
Investigating Alternatives to Nursing Homes

When an older person begins to lose the ability to manage independently, concerned relatives too often think of only two options: either assuming the responsibility of total care themselves or placing the older person in a nursing home. In practical terms, the first option is not a realistic possibility for many families today. Some of the circumstances that made it natural for adult children to care for their ailing parents in more traditional societies do not exist today. For more than a generation, housing has been built for the nuclear family, not for extended families. With increasing numbers of women entering the work force, the majority of households no longer have a full-time primary caretaker who could provide all the services an elderly parent in failing health might need. In addition, the habits of independent living, formed over so many years, can be extremely difficult to break, for aging parents as well as for their children. Although the majority of Americans may still feel a traditional sense of filial responsibility that tells them that they *should* take their aging parents into their own homes, many simply cannot, and many older people would vastly prefer not to be dependent on their children in any case.

For a number of years, the sad result of changing American life patterns was that many older people and their families had no alternative to nursing home placement once the aging relatives could no longer take care of themselves. Fortunately, in recent years, as the elderly have become an increasingly large and vocal part of the American populace, both the public and the private sectors of the medical community have been recognizing and responding to a need for other forms of assistance. As a result, many new facilities and services have been developed, from special housing projects to adult day health care centers, that offer a wide range of alternatives to elderly people who can no longer manage entirely on their own. The American Public Health Association has estimated that more than 50 percent of current nursing home residents could continue to live independent lives if they were provided with adequate supportive services. The major goal of most of these recent programs has been to keep elderly people out of institutions for as long as possible by providing them with a community-based continuum of supportive services that will allow them to remain in their own homes and communities, close to their families and friends.

Comprehensive community programs for the elderly include far more than medical and health care services. They offer as well a wide range of supportive services to meet the residential, homemaking, social, emotional and nutritional needs of older people.

A widow who has become increasingly depressed and apathetic in the isolation of her own home since the death of her husband may find new friends and interests in a congregate housing complex for the elderly. With the availability of in-home nursing and housekeeping services, a man recovering from a stroke may be able to remain in his own home.

If you are not absolutely certain that your relative requires the round-the-clock nursing care that a skilled nursing home provides, you should investigate the alternatives your community has to offer. Until the necessity arises, most people have no idea of the range and number of supportive programs for the elderly that have recently sprung up in their communities. To help you begin exploring possible alternatives to nursing home placement for your older relative, this chapter describes the various kinds of facilities, programs and services—from home health services to sheltered housing—that have been designed to keep older people out of institutions for as long as possible. Although you may not find all of these services available in your parents' community, advance knowledge of all the possibilities will help you focus your search for the most appropriate kind of care for your relative.

The alternative programs fall into three categories: in-home and day care services that provide some nursing and custodial care; alternative living arrangements that allow for more independence than traditional institutional settings provide; and supplementary social services that make life easier for elderly people who are living outside institutions. Not all of the programs or facilities discussed are substitutes for the intensive medical care that nursing homes provide, but experts agree that a high percentage of the people who end up in nursing homes do not need that level of care. It is precisely because the crises that lead elderly people and their families to consider nursing home placement take so many forms that such a broad spectrum of alternatives are presented here.

The availability of services and facilities for the elderly varies widely from community to community. While the majority do not yet have a comprehensive continuum of services, new programs are constantly being developed while others change or merge in response to the needs of this growing segment of the population.

The most efficient way to begin your exploration of the alternative programs in your community is by contacting the central social services agency in your area. Nearly every area of the country now has the special information and referral services they need. Your local office should be listed in the white pages of your telephone book under "Information and Referral," or under your state or community Department of Social Services.

Although these offices are set up to handle the entire range of community services, they tend to be sensitive to the particular needs of the elderly. Many of them have developed to the point where they offer long-term case management, assigning a social worker to provide not only information but also extensive advising and continuing help in coordinating services.

Your local Family Service Agency, which you will find listed under this or a similar name in the white pages of your telephone book, is another excellent source of information. As with the information and referral services, the kinds of assistance they provide will vary from one community to another. They will always provide both general information and specific referrals, and they may offer more intensive counseling and long-term support for the elderly person and the family as well. If you should have difficulty locating the Family Service Agency in your parent's community, you can contact the Family Services Association of America for this information. If you live so far away from your parent that it is difficult for you to investigate the resources of his or her community, it is possible that the Family Service Agency in your own area may be able to provide you with some assistance.

Your local senior center can also provide useful information on local programs. Their staff will probably be well equipped to give you an overview of the kinds of services that your community provides for the elderly. Another informational resource is your local Area Agency on aging, specifically responsible for planning and developing services for the elderly in your region. A list of state agencies is to be found in Appendix A. Your exploration of community programs for the elderly may also include discussions with your local Social Security office, your county welfare administration or department of social services, your church or synagogue, the police department and, of course, your own network of friends and neighbors.

Advance knowledge of the kinds of programs and facilities that may be available will help to focus your own investigation of the resources your community has to offer. Once you begin your search, you will probably be pleasantly surprised to discover how many supportive services are available to older people in your area.

IN-HOME AND DAY CARE SERVICES

At their best, home health service agencies can provide a continuum of care for the elderly, coordinating the services of registered nurses, home health aides, and housekeepers to meet the particular needs of the individual. These agencies are generally community-based. They may be public or private, nonprofit or profit-making organizations. The services they offer can be grouped into three broad categories: home health care, personal care and homemaking assistance.

Home health care professionals provide both skilled nursing and restorative care. Depending upon the medical needs of the older person, registered nurses or licensed vocational nurses (who are also licensed practical nurses) can come into the home on a regular basis to assess the patient's health and to perform the treatments required, such as administering drugs, changing indwelling catheters or changing dressings. Restorative care services can bring physical therapists, occupational therapists or speech therapists into the home. Some health service agencies also offer the services of a medical social worker who can help the patient and family deal with problems associated with a medical condition and assist them in finding community resources to meet their needs.

Personal care services meet the nonmedical personal needs of older people who require some help with the activities of daily life—eating, bathing, using the toilet, dressing, grooming and walking. Home health service agencies can arrange for a home health aide to perform these functions, either as a live-in companion, if constant care is needed, or on a less intensive schedule.

Homemaker-chore services provide help in maintaining the household. An older person can arrange for a housekeeper to come regularly to cook, do laundry, shop, run errands and perform other light housekeeping duties. If more assistance is needed, a home health aide can assist with both personal care and light housekeeping chores.

For an elderly person, the great advantage of home health agencies is that, ideally, they can coordinate the services of trained personnel to produce a program of care tailored to individual needs. This program is supervised by a registered nurse or social worker who monitors the health and well-being of older people assigned to them, while responding to their changing needs. The continuum of services they provide enables many older people to remain in their own homes with all the emotional and social advantages that come with retaining that degree of independence. They can also make it easier for frail elderly people to live with their relatives, by performing some necessary health and personal care services to supplement the family's efforts.

Unfortunately, not everyone who would benefit from the services of a home health agency will be able to arrange for this kind of care. Although the numbers of these agencies have increased greatly in the past decade in response to the enormous need for the centralized, flexible services they provide, the demand for these services far exceeds the supply of home health workers. Many communities still have no home health agency, and many areas that have a number of them cannot accommodate all the requests for their services.

Even if these services are available in the community, many people will not be able to afford the amount of care they would require. The cost of in-home services varies greatly according to the status of the agencies, some of which base their charges on a sliding scale and the kinds and intensity of services that the older person needs. Although home health care can be less expensive than institutional care in many cases, it can be far more expensive if intensive skilled nursing and rehabilitative services are required for an extended period of time.

Although most experts and laypeople alike strongly believe that it is highly desirable to keep the elderly out of institutions for as long as possible, often neither government assistance programs nor private insurance will provide adequate reimbursement for the continuum of in-home care. Both Medicare and private insurance plans may cover part of the cost of skilled nursing care for a limited period of time, but they will not reimburse the cost of custodial or homemaking services alone. Medicaid's coverage of in-home services is as restrictive as that of Medicare, except that in most states custodial care for Medicaid-eligible elderly people is covered under Title XX of the Social Security Act.

The case of Mrs. Saunders illustrates how central a role these financial considerations can play in determining the choice between in-home services and nursing home care. When Mrs. Saunders, a recently widowed, seventy-eight-year-old former schoolteacher, suffered her first stroke, she was able to return from the hospital to her own home, aided by the spectrum of services provided by a home health agency. Most of the cost of these in-home services was covered by Medicare. After three-and-a-half months, she no longer needed the services of a nurse or a therapist, but she still required a home health aide to assist her with personal care and housekeeping. Fortunately, she could afford to pay $840 a month for a home health aide out of her own pocket, because Medicare would not reimburse her for services of this kind. After she suffered a second, more severe stroke six months later, however, she realized that she could no longer afford to pay for the services she would need to remain in her own home. Since she had already exhausted her Medicare coverage for the year, she would have to bear all the costs herself, and the total cost of a home health aide and regular visits from a nurse and a therapist plus her regular living expenses would be $2500 a month—more than $1000 a month higher than the cost of a nursing home. Although she could have led a happier, more independent life in her own home, she simply could not afford this far more costly alternative. And because her income was still much too high for her to qualify for Medicaid, she was forced to enter a nursing home, although she could hardly believe that she had no other viable choice.

If your older relative or friend is eligible for Medicare or Medicaid coverage for in-home health services, you should also be aware that these programs will reimburse only for services provided by a licensed home care agency. You should check carefully to be sure that the agency you plan to use is properly certified if you expect the government to pay part of the costs you will incur. To avoid unpleasant surprises, you should determine in advance precisely which services will be covered by Medicare or Medicaid. Licensed agencies should be able to give you this information.

Even if your community does not have a health care agency, or if the ones in your area have long waiting lists, it may still be possible, if more time-consuming and difficult, to put together a similar combination of services in other ways.

Visiting nurse services, usually supported by voluntary organizations, exist in nearly every community. Depending upon the individual's needs, registered nurses or licensed practical (or vocational) nurses will arrange regular visits to an elderly person suffering from an acute or chronic illness in order to monitor her or his health, administer special treatments, and to instruct family members and other attendants on how to provide the necessary care.

For many elderly people, regular visits from a visiting nurse provide a vital lifeline of personal support and a crucial contact with other community services. Visiting nurses' associations generally use a sliding scale of fees. Their services may or may not be covered by Medicare and Medicaid programs.

Live-in companions as well as daytime attendants or housekeepers can be found independent of health care service agencies. Most small towns and rural areas, which may not have formal health care agencies, almost invariably have an informal network of people who perform these services. Since the homemaker–home health aides provided by the agencies are not licensed and do not necessarily receive any specialized training, you may be able to find attendants who are equally competent and caring on your own. Physicians, visiting nurses, social service agencies or clergymen can be good sources of access to this informal network of caregivers. You should be aware, however, that government assistance programs will not reimburse you for the cost of these services if they are not provided by a licensed agency.

For an elderly person at home, a live-in companion can perform a number of essential services, from light housekeeping and general monitoring of daily routine to personal care, depending on the individual's needs. If only fairly light duties are required, a vigorous older person with limited means might enjoy the opportunity to share your relative's home, with a small salary to supplement other income. In a college town or urban area, students can be found to perform personal and housekeeping services in exchange for free room and board and a small salary.

Mrs. Stanford, for example, was in her late seventies and recovering from a brief hospital stay. Her eyesight was failing, but she wanted to maintain her independence. A friend of the family recommended Florence, a woman in her fifties who was anxious to reduce her own living expenses. Mrs. Stanford and her daughter interviewed Florence, and they decided to hire her. Florence received free room and board and a small weekly salary. In exchange, she helped with cooking and dishwashing, did some shopping and was home evenings and weekends. This arrangement worked well for all concerned. Florence was able to continue her job as a salesclerk while supplementing her low pay with the free room and board and the additional salary. Mrs. Stanford still had time to herself and could entertain friends in the afternoons. In the evenings, she had a pleasant companion and some extra help. The family was reassured by knowing that someone was with their mother to help her along.

If Mrs. Stanford had also needed some nursing care, her companion's services could have been supplemented by regular short visits from a nurse. If she had required round-the-clock assistance, of course, her family would have had to find an attendant who had no other employment and pay her a much larger salary. Constant nursing care can be prohibitively expensive, but when what is required is primarily help with personal care and housekeeping, these services can often be brought into the home at a lower cost and with a far greater level of emotional satisfaction than a nursing home could offer. Especially if you cannot rely on the centralized services of a home health service agency, putting together a program of care for your relative will take creative thinking, sustained inquiries, thoughtful interviewing and careful supervision, but the benefits to the older person and the entire family can be well worth the effort required.

ADULT DAY HEALTH PROGRAMS

One of the most exciting recent developments in health care for the elderly is the adult day health programs, which provide a range of health, social and supportive services in community-based centers to care for disabled or seriously ill elderly persons. In 1970, the federal government funded four experimental programs of this kind. Since then, their numbers have increased well over a hundredfold and many more new programs are being planned and funded every year. Their primary purpose is to offer a range of health care and supportive services that will enable many older people to avoid institutionalization.

Day health centers provide a range of services, including screening for medical conditions, medical and nursing care, physical, occupational and speech therapy, social work, recreational therapy, personal care (bathing, grooming), educational programs, crafts, meals and transportation. Unlike senior centers, day health services are not available on a drop-in basis. A person who participates in the program is scheduled to attend the center for a specified number of days per week depending upon his or her need for services. Most centers have a multidisciplinary assessment team, composed of a physician, a nurse, a therapist and a social worker, that determines the range and level of services required by a participant and then prepares a treatment plan that is reevaluated on a regular basis. Day health centers are generally small, providing fifteen to twenty-five participants with six to eight hours of care each day. They can be located in a variety of settings—schools, churches, nursing homes, hospitals or independent facilities.

Whether an older person is living alone or with family members, a program of this kind can prove extremely beneficial. In addition to providing a range of medical and rehabilitative services, it also creates an ongoing support group, composed of both clients and staff, that offers the warmth and concern of an extended family. For the older person who lives alone, it affords an enjoyable alternative to the isolation and boredom of solitary living. This arrangement can also enable families to arrange for care during the hours that family members are working, and give them some relief from the constant responsibility of attending to the needs of their relative.

Usually less costly than nursing home care, adult day health programs vary in price on a per diem basis. The cost of day health services can vary, but you can expect to pay between $20 and $45 per day. Most centers have a sliding-scale fee, based on the participant's ability to pay. In some states, Medicare and Medicaid will cover the cost of services. Private insurance does not cover adult day health services at this time.

ADULT DAY CARE PROGRAMS

While adult day health care programs are designed for elderly people who are seriously ill or disabled, adult day care centers serve the needs of people who require less intensive medical services. Adult day care offers daytime supervision, health monitoring and physical therapy to older people who are somewhat frail and may need walkers or wheelchairs, but are not bedridden. In addition to health services aimed at maintaining clients' physical conditions, day care centers provide hot lunches and snacks, companionship of other clients and staff, planned recreational activities and transportation. They can be used by older people who live alone or with a nighttime companion as well as by those who live with relatives. The cost of adult day care is not covered by government assistance programs. The cost varies from $10 to $20 per day. As with other programs, many centers have a sliding-scale fee, based on the participants' ability to pay.

RESPITE CARE

Respite care, another promising recent development in the health care field, is designed to give family members some relief from the constant strain of caring for an older relative.

Some nursing homes are set up to allow an older person to stay in the institution on a temporary basis, for a week or even just for a weekend. This program can be extremely beneficial for families; knowing that respite care is available may make families feel much more willing and able to keep their older relatives at home for extended periods of time.

The cost for respite care is approximately $75 per day or more. Private insurance may cover this kind of care, and in some states, Medicare and Medicaid will reimburse part of the cost.

HOSPICE CARE

Another relatively new concept in the health care field, hospice programs provide for the emotional as well as the medical needs of terminally ill patients and their families by offering a range of supportive services that are not readily available in conventional hospital and skilled nursing facilities. Designed for people for whom active therapeutic treatment is no longer being pursued because it is no longer deemed appropriate, hospice programs emphasize care and comfort, not rehabilitation. Hospice care embraces both the older person and the family, and the services it provides extend through the bereavement period.

The first program of this type in the United States was established in 1974. Since then, many such projects have been developed and many more are being planned. At this stage, few hospice programs in the country provide a comprehensive range of services (home care, day care, night care, respite care and inpatient care). Some offer only counseling services to patients in hospitals, in nursing homes or at home. Others provide a multidisciplinary hospice team in an existing inpatient facility. A few programs have independent facilities specifically designed to care for the terminally ill in a homelike environment. Depending upon the services provided by the program, the cost can range from $40 to $90 per day. Medicare or private insurance may cover part of the cost. Quite often a fund is set up through the hospice program that will help patients with expenses.

RESIDENTIAL ALTERNATIVES TO SKILLED NURSING HOMES

Continuing care facilities, sometimes called multilevel homes, combine a wide range of living accommodations and supportive services, from independent apartments or cottages to skilled nursing facilities, within a single retirement community. In addition to a central dining and social area, these complexes often include game and craft rooms, a library and an auditorium. They generally offer a range of recreational and cultural activities, such as exercise classes, dancing, programs on current events, travelogues and organized trips.

Residents usually enter these communities while they are still healthy and vigorous enough to live in their own units and take advantage of the recreational and social opportunities that make these living arrangements so appealing. The major attraction of these facilities, however, is that they ease the crises of failing health by making available a full range of supportive services, from housekeeping and personal assistance to intensive nursing care, if and when it is needed.

Because the focus of these facilities is on providing lifetime care, they require long-term contracts and substantial entrance fees, ranging from $10,000 to $100,000 or more. In addition to this one time fee, residents also pay a monthly charge to cover maintenance, meals (although these may be optional) and other basic expenses. These monthly fees begin at $500 for a single person and $900 for a couple. They can be expected to increase as the cost-of-living index rises. Most homes that charge a high initial fee have included future health care costs in that figure, while those with a relatively low entrance fee generally assess a substantial additional monthly charge for nursing care.

Because the combination of independence and security that these facilities provide has proven to be extremely attractive to elderly people who can afford them, the number of continuing care homes has been growing rapidly in recent years. By now there are more than four hundred such communities scattered across the country. The American Association of Homes for the Aging (1050 17th Street, N.W., Washington, D.C. 20036) can provide you with a list of them. Because the existing facilities barely begin to meet the current demand, you may have to wait as long as five years for a vacancy.

Since these homes require such a large initial investment, you should thoroughly investigate the financial stability of the organization before you commit your future security to its care. Although most of these homes are financially sound, some problems have arisen and a few have been forced into bankruptcy, leaving their residents in an unfortunate situation. In addition, you should be sure to review all the community's rules and regulations, which can be quite extensive, and have your lawyer and accountant look over the details of the contract.

Residential care homes, also described as domiciliary care facilities, personal care homes or board and care homes, offer a protective environment for elderly people who are no longer able to live independently in the community.

Each resident has a furnished private or shared room and receives three meals a day. Some homes provide special diets. The homes also have some responsibility for personal care, offering help with bathing, dressing, showering, eating and walking, if necessary. They provide no nursing or rehabilitative services, although the homes' operators can dispense medications according to a doctor's instructions. These homes will generally furnish transportation for medical appointments and other errands and offer some recreational activities during the day.

Because these homes generally offer round-the-clock supervision, they can serve as an alternative to nursing homes for older people who can no longer prepare their own meals and require assistance with personal care, but who do not need the intensive medical attention and round-the-clock nursing care that nursing homes provide. Older people who do not require that kind of medical treatment will probably prefer the smaller, more home-like setting of a residential care home to the institutional atmosphere of a nursing home.

There are no federal regulations governing these homes, but they are usually licensed by state departments of social services, which establish criteria for the physical facilities and the types of services to be provided.

The cost of residential care varies, but you can expect to pay $500 a month or more. Medicare and private insurance do not cover the cost of residential care. Elderly people with low incomes who qualify for Supplemental Security Income (SSI), however, can receive substantial cash assistance for this type of housing. If you believe your older relative may qualify for SSI, check with the county welfare office.

It should be noted that there is a current trend to combine, but still have in separate quarters, residential care and long-term care facilities. The idea is to assist the frail elderly residents who might need help in dressing, eating, bathing, etc., but who are still independent.

Congregate or sheltered housing serves elderly people who need some assistance in order to continue to live on their own but who do not require the kinds of custodial services that a residential care home provides. These facilities are apartment complexes designed especially for older people. Some have specially equipped apartments for the handicapped, with special provisions for wheelchairs. Usually these complexes provide some meals, served in a communal dining room, and make available housekeeping and transportation services. Frequently, a congregate housing complex will also have a number of health, social and recreational programs for its residents. Older people can use the services they need while retaining their independence.

Congregate housing is an excellent arrangement for someone who wants security and companionship in pleasant surroundings and immediate access to the range of health and supportive services it provides. These complexes are frequently sponsored by church organizations or community groups, although some are run by private investors, and the government funds a limited number of programs for the low-income elderly.

The cost of congregate housing will vary with the type of facility and the number of services a person uses. You can expect to pay $400 per month or more for this type of housing. Government programs charge a sliding-scale fee for services, based on the resident's income, and some projects are subsidized.

Senior apartments are especially designed for elderly people who have both the desire and the ability to live independent lives. Many of these places offer dining and housekeeping services for those who need some assistance in these areas.

Shared homes. Many elderly people find themselves living alone after the death of a spouse. For those whose health is reasonably good, sharing their home with another person can be an excellent solution, giving them both companionship and help in case of an emergency.

Especially because the family home is the only substantial asset that many older people have at their disposal, extra living space can often be traded for help with cooking, household chores, or other tasks of daily life. If properly chosen, "roommates" can considerably enhance the quality of older people's lives, giving them not only an additional sense of security, but also the emotional warmth and the new interests that come with making a new friend.

Communal living is an arrangement in which a number of people live together and pool expenses. For elderly people who

REIMBURSEMENT FOR HEALTH SERVICES

SERVICE[1]	MEDICARE	MEDICAID	PRIVATE INSURANCE
Extended Care Facility	100 days/yr.	None	Limited or None
Skilled Nursing Facility	100 days/yr.	Unlimited Coverage	Limited or None
Intermediate Care Facility	None	Unlimited Coverage	None
In-Home Services			
Skilled (nursing, therapy, etc.)	100 days/yr.	Varies from state to state, but usually as restrictive as Medicare[2]	Limited or None
Custodial (personal care and (homemaking)	100 days/yr. (if skilled care in required)		
Adult Day Health	A few states cover	Approx. 10 states cover this	None
Congregate Housing			
Private	None	None	None
Government[3]	None	None	None
Residential Care Homes[4]	None	None	None
Hospice Care	80% of total costs	None	Limited or None
Respite Care	A few states cover	A few states cover	None

[1]None of the other alternatives discussed in the book are covered under Medicare, Medicaid or private insurance.

[2]In most states, custodial care for Medicaid-eligible persons is covered under Title XX of the Social Security Act (Social Services). This money provides services for the elderly who do not require skilled in-home care, but do need custodial care on a continuing basis. (Often called in-home supportive services).

[3]The Department of Housing and Urban Development has a special program that subsidizes services and the cost of housing in congregate housing projects.

[4]Low-income elderly living in personal care homes who qualify for Supplemental Security Income (SSI) can receive substantial cash assistance for this type of housing.

are unable or unwilling to live alone in an apartment or a hotel, this kind of group living can be an excellent alternative.

Mr. Diaz, a retired contractor on a fixed income, had lived alone in an apartment since the death of his wife. When he was seventy-five, the latest rent increase forced him to think about making some changes in his life. Although the senior center provided him with great pleasure and companionship during the day, he was lonely in the evening. He discovered that some of his friends at the center were in the same situation, and the idea of living together appealed to them. Mr. Diaz and five friends were able to lease a large home in a convenient location. The senior center helped them organized the details, including the do's and don'ts of living together. The beneficial results in this instance were companionship, a greater interest in meals, a family feeling of concern for one another and reduced expenses for each individual.

OTHER SUPPORTIVE SERVICES

Most communities have a variety of other supportive services for elderly people. While the programs discussed in this section are not specifically aimed at meeting the housing or health care needs of older people, the additional assistance they provide makes it easier for the elderly to lead independent lives.

Senior centers have been established in almost every community. They usually provide hot lunches as well as a range of educational and recreational activities for older people. In addition, they frequently serve as an excellent source of information concerning other community resources for the elderly.

Meals-on-Wheels, as home-delivered meals programs are frequently called, provides nutritious meals five days a week to the homebound elderly. In some areas, this service is available on weekends as well.

Mental health services. Many older people experience some emotional problems as part of the aging process. Declining health and the loss of spouse and friends can cause extreme anxiety or severe depression. Most areas have community mental health or psychiatric clinics staffed by trained social workers, psychologists and psychiatrists. Some have programs designed specifically for the elderly.

Protective services are designed to assist older people who are no longer able to take care of their personal affairs and have no family or friends to help. Depending upon the situation, these agencies can provide a conservator to monitor the person's needs or a conservator of the estate to manage financial affairs.

Legal services for the elderly can assist in circumstances such as eviction, public assistance difficulties, property losses, involuntary commitments and consumer problems.

Telephone reassurance programs are quite often the only lifeline to the outside world for the elderly living alone. This program arranges for a daily phone call by a volunteer or by a telephone checking service to be sure that all is well.

Postal alert is designed for the frail elderly who are living alone. A sign at their mailbox states: "If my mail is stacking up, please call the police department so that they can check on my welfare."

Senior escort and transportation programs serve the needs of older people who are fearful for their personal safety outside their own homes. They are usually staffed by volunteers who escort the elderly on errands and visits.

Roving patrols serve the elderly living in high-crime areas. They run errands, make note of safety hazards and try to prevent attacks on the elderly. These civilian employees of the police department walk the streets, carry walkie-talkies and wear regulation jackets so as to be easily identified.

ARRANGING A PROGRAM OF CARE

Arranging for a combination of community-based services can be more complex and time-consuming than simply entering a nursing home where all the necessary services are provided under one roof. While some older people may prefer the simplicity and security of nursing home care, in many cases the emotional rewards of more independent living, for both the elderly and their families, will amply repay the time and effort it takes to establish and monitor a program of care tailored to individual needs.

If you or your relative decide to try to design an alternative program of care, you can expect to receive a great deal of help and support from the professionals who staff community-based services for the elderly. Once you have decided which local facilities and services may be appropriate, the next step is to make an appointment for you and your relative to meet with the director. If you are contacting one of the more health-oriented programs—a home health service agency, an adult day health center or a congregate housing project—a team of professionals will probably make an initial assessment of the older person's health and functional status.

If a single program cannot meet all of the elderly person's needs, as is often the case, health care professionals may be able to direct you to other community services that provide the necessary supplementary assistance. A man recovering from a stroke, for example, may need an adult day health center three days a week to monitor his medical condition and give him physical and speech therapy; a home health aide six hours a week, to help him with personal care and household tasks; Meals-on-Wheels to ensure adequate nutrition; and a telephone reassurance program to give him a sense of security on weekends.

Other organizations may also be able to help you arrange a community-based program of care. If the older person is currently hospitalized, the hospital discharge planner may be able to help you. Information and Referral or your local Family Service Agency may be able to offer you a professional counselor who can help you put together the right combination of services for your relative. It is possible that you may have to assume the role of coordinator yourself.

The development of supportive services for the elderly has been far from uniform across the country. Some locales offer a wide range of programs and facilities while others still have very few. A frail widow who lives in an isolated rural area may find no viable alternative to nursing home placement, while a woman who lives in a metropolitan or suburban area may find the supportive services that will enable her to live at home with the same disability.

If you live at a distance from your ailing parent or other relative, you may wish to explore the resources of your own community as well as those of hers or his before your family reaches its decision. Health care professionals agree that it is generally desirable for elderly people to remain in their own community, either in their own home, as long as that is possible, or in a nearby nursing home, so that they can remain in touch with a familiar environment and, even more important, with their friends or the people who love them. But since the most crucial and most sustained emotional support for elderly people usually comes from close relatives, those families in which the children no longer live close to their parent face the difficult question of where the older person will be more comfortable—in familiar surroundings or close to the children, where there is sustained emotional support. If you discover that there are striking differences between the range and quality of supportive services offered by the relative's community and yours, this knowledge could prove to be critical in deciding which location is best for the future.

After investigating all the alternatives, your family may still come to the conclusion that a nursing home is the only workable solution. Even if this is the case, the time all of you have spent in exploring, discussing and, finally, discarding other options will not have been in vain. At least the entire family, and especially the older person, will be satisfied that they have investigated every possible alternative before deciding that only a nursing home will provide the kind of care needed. The conclusion may be no less painful for all concerned, but the feelings of guilt and resentment that so often accompany this decision will be greatly diminished.

3

Selecting a Nursing Home

Statistics show that three out of every ten people over sixty-five years of age will enter a nursing home, for an average stay of two and a half years. Even with the alternative forms of care that are now available, many families will eventually need to find a nursing home for their relative. Although it is far from pleasant to contemplate this possibility before it becomes an unavoidable necessity, families who have planned in advance will find themselves far better equipped to deal with it than those who are suddenly faced with the need for immediate action.

From a purely practical point of view, many nursing homes have long waiting lists. If you wait until the last possible moment to confront this possibility, you may be forced to find a nursing home, any nursing home, in a hurry. By planning ahead, you will be able to locate the best possible institution and ensure that it can accommodate your relative when the time comes. It will also allow him or her an active role in this major life decision.

The thousands of nursing homes in this country today present a wide range of choices. Some are small, serving as few as fifteen residents, while others care for 250 or more clients. Some are sponsored by nonprofit church or ethnic groups; others are run by profit-making corporations. Both the kinds and the quality of care these institutions provide vary considerably from one home to another. Some are excellent, while others leave much to be desired. In some areas, there are many homes to choose from; in others, the choices are more limited.

The first step in the process of finding the right nursing home is to survey the options available in the community. If your relative will be entering a nursing home directly from a hospital, the discharge planner or social services director can furnish you with a list of those in the area. The office of your local Long-Term Care Ombudsman program, a government agency that has access to all long-term care facilities, can give you useful information about the homes in your area. (Because this agency quite frequently takes its name from the community in which it is located, it can be difficult to find. Information and Referral can direct you to the Long-Term Care Ombudsman that serves your area, and Appendix A lists the central office of the Long-Term Care Ombudsman program for every state.) A list of accredited homes can be obtained from the American Association of Homes for the Aging (A.A.H.A.), your state affiliate of the American Health Care Association (A.H.C.A.) or the local medical society or health department. In addition, many local Information and Referral services and other social service agencies provide lists of approved nursing homes in the area. Some areas even have nursing home placement services that, for a fee charged to the home, will assist families in locating the kind of care their older relatives need. Clergymen, many of whom are well acquainted with local institutions, may also be of assistance, and friends and neighbors who are familiar with one or more homes in the area can help. It is also possible that the older person's doctor or your own physician may be willing to give you his personal evaluation of various nursing homes in the area.

While professionals and friends can help you draw up and

perhaps limit your list of options, the final choice of the best possible nursing home will be your family's and the prospective resident's responsibility. The more you know about what to look for and what to look out for, the more confident you will feel about your ability to make the right decision when the time comes.

BASIC FACTS ABOUT NURSING HOMES TODAY

Before you begin to evaluate the nursing homes in your area, you will need to become familiar with a number of fundamental issues that will help to focus your initial inquiries. Knowing the right questions to ask will make your preliminary survey of the institutions on your list both more efficient and more effective.

Sponsorship

Today, approximately 75 percent of American nursing homes are privately owned profit-making institutions, commonly labeled proprietary homes. Twenty percent are voluntary, sponsored by nonprofit organizations that may be either sectarian or nonsectarian. The rest, a very small number, are public, government-sponsored institutions.

During the past decade, both the number and the size of privately owned profit-making homes have increased greatly. Many are now run by large corporations that have chains of homes throughout the country. In evaluating homes of this kind, you should be aware of the potential conflict between providing quality care and running a profitable business, but you should not necessarily assume that their services will be inferior to those provided by nonprofit homes. You might find that some privately owned homes are excellent and some nonprofit institutions are inferior in quality.

While the kind of sponsorship an institution has is not necessarily a guarantee of the quality of care it provides, it may well help to determine the kind of clients it attracts and the cultural atmosphere it maintains. If religion has always been an important part of your relative's life, she or he may strongly prefer a church- or synagogue-sponsored home. A number of ethnic and fraternal organizations also sponsor nonprofit homes for their elderly. In cases like these, the sponsorship of a home can be extremely important in making an older person feel comfortable and secure in a new environment.

Levels of Care

Not all of the institutions that laypeople call nursing homes provide the same kinds of care. Federal laws regulating Medicare and Medicaid benefits have established three categories of nursing home facilities, determined by the level of medical services they provide.

Extended Care Facilities

Especially designed for patients, not necessarily elderly, who need short-term convalescent care after being discharged from a hospital, extended care facilities serve only patients who are expected to recover fully from their illnesses or injuries. The services they provide include intensive rehabilitative programs as well as medical care, twenty-four-hour skilled nursing care, counseling and a range of other supportive services. Because the government defines eligibility for this level of care so narrowly, there are few of these independent facilities in operation, although skilled nursing homes sometimes offer this service as an option.

Skilled Nursing Facilities

These days the great majority of nursing homes are skilled nursing facilities, designed to serve residents who require skilled nursing care on a long-term basis. These are medical institutions designed to care for those men and women who are severely ill but who do not require the constant availability of specialized medical services that hospitals provide. Under federal regulations, skilled nursing homes must offer twenty-four-hour nursing care, medical, dietary and pharmaceutical services, and activity programs. They must also arrange to provide any prescribed medical services by bringing in contract personnel or by transporting the resident to a nearby health facility if no one on the staff is qualified to perform the necessary services.

Intermediate Care Facilities

Designed for residents who require only a minimum level of health care, these facilities provide less professional staffing and fewer medical services than the skilled nursing facilities. Their services are primarily geared to personal, nutritional and social needs, not to medical care or rehabilitation. Aides give residents the custodial assistance they need for the routine activities of daily life—dressing, bathing, grooming, eating, using the toilet.

Multilevel Facilities

Many nursing homes offer two different levels of care under one roof. In a skilled nursing home, for example, ten beds out of two hundred could be designated as an extended care facility. One wing of a home may be an intermediate care facility, while the rest is devoted to skilled nursing care. This arrangement can be highly desirable because it allows an older person to enter a home as an intermediate care patient and make an easy transition to a higher level of care if this becomes necessary.

Unfortunately, however, intermediate care facilities are becoming harder to find as more and more nursing homes find it economically more advantageous to offer only skilled nursing care, for which they can charge a significantly higher daily rate.

Staffing

The composition of nursing home staffs varies considerably depending upon the type and size of the home. Large Medicare/Medicaid–certified skilled nursing homes may employ a medical director and staff physicians, licensed dieticians, physical therapists and social workers on a full-time basis, while smaller homes contract for these and other services on a part-time or consulting basis. Whereas federal laws mandate that a wide range of medical and therapeutic services must be made available to Medicare or Medicaid patients who require them, even in larger homes many of these are generally performed by outside consultants rather than by full-time staff members.

In federally certified facilities, all medical services are coordinated and supervised by a medical director, who must be a licensed physician or osteopath. Each resident has an attending physician who is responsible for planning and monitoring his or her treatment and rehabilitation programs and reviewing progress on at least a monthly basis. While the medical director can serve as a resident's attending physician, the patient or his or her relatives should be free to choose the physician who will oversee the medical care and to change doctors if the need arises. Some nursing homes expect residents to choose their attending physician from a list of its staff physicians. Even if this is the case, however, most homes will allow an outside physician to apply for staff membership.

Federal and state regulations dictate both the composition and size of the nursing staff. In a skilled nursing facility, a registered nurse must be on duty twenty-four hours a day. In an intermediate care facility, a licensed vocational nurse can supervise the work of aides and orderlies.

In any nursing home, however, it is the orderlies and aides who are responsible for at least 80 to 90 percent of the residents' daily care. Nearly every state has a specified ratio of aides and orderlies to residents—usually about three staff hours per resident per day—as part of its licensing requirements.

A word of caution is in order here. A large staff with good credentials does not necessarily mean that a home provides high-quality care to its residents. Because the aides and orderlies are the ones who spend the most time with the residents, their competence and, above all, their attitudes will be the most crucial factors in your relative's daily nursing home life. To evaluate the quality of daily personal care that residents receive, there is no substitute for your own observations during a number of visits.

Costs and Financing

As I mentioned earlier, you can expect a skilled nursing home to charge $1200* a month or more, and intermediate care facilities start at $900 a month. The assistance you can anticipate from Medicare, Medicaid and private insurance plans has already been covered under ''The Financial Facts'' (pp. 8–14). It should be stressed, however, that families and their older relative should be absolutely sure that the home they choose is both certified for and will accept Medicare and Medicaid payments. And they should be sure they understand that these payments may be substantially lower than the fees many homes charge their privately funded residents. You should also take a hard look at your relative's financial situation and make sure

*Metropolitan Life Insurance Company, ''News Watch,'' *Geriatric Nursing,* March/April 1986, pp. 64–65.

you understand what type of government assistance is available now and in the future.

Homes that accept only privately funded residents are under no obligation to continue providing care for a person who cannot pay the bill. If a resident's resources are exhausted and the home does not accept Medicaid payments, he or she will have to leave. Some homes that accept Medicare residents will not care for those funded by Medicaid, although nonprofit homes are required by law to accept Medicaid residents whenever possible to maintain their favored tax status.

Specific cases encountered by the author indicate that with the ever-widening gap between the fees nursing homes can demand from residents who pay their own way and the level of Medicaid reimbursement, many nursing homes are refusing to accept Medicaid residents, even though they are certified to provide these services. It has long been the case that many Medicaid-certified homes refuse to accept new residents who cannot pay for at least some period of care from their own funds. We have seen firsthand that it is not uncommon for nursing homes certified by Medicaid to evict residents once they have exhausted their own resources and are forced to apply for government assistance.

On the other hand, some homes do incorporate residents who pay privately with Medicaid residents. Consequently, because changing from one nursing home to another places such great strain on frail elderly people, it is important to make sure that you know what the nursing home's policy is before you make a choice.

Licensing, Certification and Accreditation

Today, the nursing home industry is regulated by a battery of government regulations and ordinances that range from building design to service delivery. The federal government dictates the overall regulative structure, and states enforce specific codes for operation. All nursing homes are subject to state licensing and inspection. Federal regulations, which are often but not always more stringent than those of the states, are enforced through the Medicare and Medicaid programs: only those facilities that meet federal government standards can accept Medicare or Medicaid patients.

Only institutions that are federally certified under the Medicare and Medicaid programs can legally call themselves *skilled* nursing homes, but you should bear in mind that what the administrators/owners of a home call it does not necessarily indicate its licensing status or the range and quality of services it provides.

In your survey of local facilities, one of the first facts you should check is their licensing status. If the home is not both state licensed and certified as a provider of Medicare and Medicaid, you should be particularly cautious in evaluating the quality of care it provides. Although excellent homes have chosen to accept only privately funded residents, either to avoid the red tape of federal regulation or because their customary fees are higher than the level of government reimbursement, it could also be the case that a home does not participate in these programs because it has failed to meet federal and state standards.

State and federal laws provide for a number of actions that can be taken against nursing homes that violate regulations. Homes that fail to meet government standards can be either fined or closed down. In the case of homes that do not participate in Medicare or Medicaid, the state licensing agency can revoke their business licenses and prohibit them from operating. As a less drastic measure, a home may be granted only a provisional license if it has a number of violations that do not substantially endanger the lives or safety of its residents. In these cases, the problems must be remedied within a specified period of time before a permanent license will be granted.

Unfortunately, the fact that a nursing home is properly licensed by the state and certified by the federal government does not necessarily ensure that the care it provides will be of high quality. During the author's many visits to nursing homes, it was noted that the current inspection system has a number of shortcomings, not the least of which is an inadequate budget and staff. Inspections serve both to evaluate the physical plant and to monitor the quality of care the residents receive. Because of the shortage of nursing home space in many areas and the traumatic effects of relocation on residents, officials generally hesitate to take strong action until they see flagrant abuses.

A more reliable and more exacting evaluation of the quality of nursing home care is conducted by a nongovernmental agency. The American Health Care Association's Quest for Quality Program is closely linked with the state inspection and requires that the staff take classes approved by AHCA. If you find a home that has won the approval of this organization, you can feel confident that your relative will receive high-quality treatment there.

NARROWING YOUR OPTIONS

Once you have assembled a preliminary list of the nursing homes available in the geographical area of your choice, you can use the telephone to begin collecting information that will help you eliminate some and focus on the ones that seem most appropriate for your older relative's or friend's needs and circumstances. These days many homes will send you brochures and other promotional materials that provide some facts about their operations as well as some sense of the appearance of their physical plants.

Here are the most important questions to keep in mind when you make your initial inquiries:

- What level of care does the home provide? Is it a skilled nursing facility, an intermediate care facility, or a combination of the two?
- Is it licensed by the state? Is it certified for Medicare and Medicaid?
- Has it won approval by the American Health Care Association in its Quest for Quality Program?
- What is its sponsorship? Is it private? Nonprofit? If it is nonprofit, is it sectarian or nonsectarian? What is the sponsoring organization?
- Is the location convenient?
- How many beds does it have?
- What are the daily costs?
- Does it accept Medicaid patients? How does it treat private patients who are later forced to go on Medicaid?
- Will there be a vacancy at the time your older relative will need to enter a home?

If you have sought the advice of social workers, physicians or other knowledgeable people in the community, their recommendations may help you to steer away from some homes and to think favorably of others, especially if you hear the same opinions expressed by a number of people.

CONDUCTING YOUR OWN EVALUATION

Once you have narrowed your options to the two or three nursing homes that seem most suitable for your loved one in terms of location, level of care, costs and accreditation, you should plan to conduct your own thorough inspection of each one before you make your final choice. Nursing home administrators will be glad to arrange a guided tour of their facilities if you call in advance for an appointment. While this official tour is an important first step in shaping your impressions of a home, it is only the beginning of a comprehensive personal evaluation. It is your role, as an active consumer as well as advocate for your older relative, to visit each home with your own criteria clearly in mind.

If you are well prepared for your visits, you can use these opportunities to observe a multitude of details and to gather all the information you will need to evaluate the quality of care each home provides. Because the administrator establishes and implements the policies that most directly affect the daily life of the residents, the attitudes he or she reveals while showing you the home and responding to your questions will leave you with a strong impression of the personality and priorities that guide the institution.

A good administrator should be willing to help you investigate every area of nursing home life that will affect the physical and emotional welfare of the prospective resident. The administrator and the staff should respond competently and sensitively to all your questions and allow you to speak freely with other staff members and residents.

If you are impressed by what you see and hear on your guided tour, you may wish to return, unannounced, at a different time of day to observe another part of the home's daily routine. A morning tour could be followed by an informal visit at dinnertime to observe the food service and evening recreational activities of the home. Although of course you cannot enter residents' living quarters uninvited, you have the right, once you have signed in, to visit dining rooms, lounges and other public areas on your own and chat with the residents and staff members you encounter there.

If at all possible, the older person who will soon become a resident in one of these homes should have some role in evaluating the alternatives. Exactly what that role should be depends upon the personality and emotional state as well as the physical condition of the individual. You may feel freer to conduct a rigorous evaluation if you are not accompanied by your relative on the visits that serve this purpose, especially if she or he is already apprehensive about the prospect of entering a nursing home. In this case, you may choose to conduct your own inspection first and then take your relative to visit only those homes that you have found satisfactory. This would allow you to separate the cautious, watchful attitude that is necessary for a critical evaluation from the positive presentation of alternatives that the prospective resident may need at this difficult time.

If you have never ventured inside a nursing home until this time, as many people have not, you will need to brace yourself for the initial shock you will inevitably experience on your first visit. Nowhere except in a nursing home is there such a concentration of infirm elderly people, and the first sight of any nursing home population can be unsettling. If you don't sufficiently prepare yourself for the fact that this is what you will encounter in any nursing home, you may end up seeing nothing else. Many people find it difficult to evaluate the quality of life within that framework, and several trips might be necessary to acquire a balanced perspective.

Licensing and Inspection Reports

During your first visit, if you have not yet done so, you should take the opportunity to check the licensing status of the nursing home and of its key personnel. Most states require that the administrator and the director of nursing have professional licenses. These licenses, as well as any certificates of accreditation by the American Health Care Association's Quest for Quality Program, should be inspected to make certain that they are current and valid.

The law requires that the government inspectors' most recent report be posted in a prominent place. A careful review of this report will tell you a great deal about the quality of care a home provides. All nursing homes certified to participate in Medicare and Medicaid programs are evaluated with a federal government form entitled "Statement of Deficiencies and Plan of Correction." Standard throughout the fifty states, these forms are completed by state inspectors under federal contract. Homes that do not receive federal funding are evaluated only with state inspection forms, which vary from state to state.

Here is a sampling of the kinds of violations that inspectors have noted in their reports on various homes:

- A toothbrush was found in a resident's bedpan.
- Cockroach infestation was quite evident.
- After their showers, five residents, covered in sheets and seated in showerchairs, were tied together by a rope and pulled down the hallway by an aide to their respective rooms.
- Five residents called for help from their rooms, and staff members failed to answer or investigate.
- Residents in their rooms were in need of reposturing in their wheelchairs. Many staff members seemed oblivious to the situation; some even looked at residents while passing by and did nothing.
- Nurse-call extension cords were not readily available to residents.
- Five residents had no medical records even though they had been at the home for an average of one week.
- Five of the fifteen residents' medical records reviewed indicated a marked change of weight, and there was no documentation that the physician had been notified.
- Six of the eighteen residents' medical records reviewed did not contain documentation that physicians had been notified as to the appearance, stage and size of decubiti (bedsores).
- A review of twelve closed medical records of residents discharged to an acute care hospital in a three-month period indicated a high incidence of staph infection. Each of these residents had open lesions that originated in the home.

Reports on poorly run homes may list numerous serious violations. Even the best facilities may have a few minor ones. As you can see, it is of the utmost importance to review these documents thoroughly because it stands to reason that the better homes have better reports.

The Physical Plant

Attractive surroundings undoubtedly boost the morale of residents and are obviously an essential element in a well-run nursing home. Because what you are looking for is a *home* for someone very dear to you, an atmosphere of comfort is far more important than impeccable interior decoration. Bedrooms that clearly display the divergent tastes and interests of their residents can seem less attractive than those in which every detail conforms to a single tasteful decorating scheme. But the comforting presence of a few familiar objects may make elderly residents far happier than the most attractive institutional decor ever could.

In any nursing home, the physical plant is designed, above all, for the comfort, safety and convenient access of its residents. As you tour each home, you should keep in mind the particular health and safety requirements of elderly, infirm residents. Carpeting, for example, may seem to be an attractive decorative feature, but it can be a health and safety hazard in a nursing home. It makes walking more dangerous for elderly residents who tend to shuffle rather than lift their feet, and it traps dust and pollen that can aggravate allergies. These days the better homes have plastic floors, not too highly polished, that are scrubbed daily.

As you look at bedrooms, hallways and bathrooms, make sure they are designed for easy access by residents in wheelchairs and those who have difficulty walking. Bedrooms, which should have at least one comfortable chair for each resident and ample lighting for reading and handiwork, should have enough space for wheelchairs to maneuver easily. Hallways should be wide enough for two wheelchairs to pass each other comfortably, with hand railings for those who need assistance in walking. Bathrooms should be equipped with assists and hand railings so that your relative, if confined to a wheelchair, can use it without the use of aides. Showers, often not part of the individual bathroom facilities, should also be checked carefully for safety and accessibility as well as cleanliness.

Because older people are particularly susceptible to infection, scrupulous cleanliness is of paramount importance. Every area of a nursing home should be clean and totally free of unpleasant odors. An effective way to check the cleaning procedures of a home is to take a careful look at beds that have recently been vacated. State laws require that bed frames as well as bedding be sterilized before being made available to another resident. If the steel rails and crossbars of a vacant bed are dusty, it is unlikely that they were steam cleaned as the law requires.

Considering the frail, vulnerable state of your relative, fire-safety precautions should also be checked during your tour of a home. Fire protection equipment should include a complete sprinkler system. Fire exits should be clearly marked, unobstructed, and wide enough to accommodate bedridden residents as well as wheelchairs. Hallways should be equipped with fire doors, and all hallways and common rooms should have emergency lighting equipment powered by an auxiliary generator. Each home should have a written emergency evacuation plan, which you may wish to check. You can also ask the local fire station for an assessment of the home's ability to cope with a serious fire. The local building department may also be able to provide you with an evaluation of the structural safety of the home in the event of fire, earthquake and any other potential natural disasters in your area.

Medical Care

Because the physician who serves as medical director of a nursing home has primary responsibility for establishing medical policy and overseeing the delivery of all medical services to the residents, his reputation in the community and especially his attitude toward geriatric patients is a key indicator of the quality of medical care an institution provides. You are unlikely to be able to arrange meetings with the medical directors of the homes you are considering during your inspection tours, because the great majority of them hold only part-time posts in nursing homes. Still, it is well worth your time to try to find out all you can about this key figure from your own physician and other sources in the community.

While you are touring the home, be sure to discuss the issue of the prospective resident's attending physician with the administrator. If you have not already done so, you should make certain at this time that your relative's personal physician can serve as his or her attending physician in the nursing home.

If specialized medical or therapeutic services are required, you should also ask what arrangements the home has for making them available to the residents. You may wish to have the patient's own physician check the nursing home's list of staff consultants to be sure it meets with his or her approval.

Rehabilitation Therapy

Skilled nursing homes commonly provide three kinds of therapy programs: physical therapy, speech therapy and occupational therapy. If one or more of these has been prescribed by your relative's physician, check whether it is offered by each of the homes you visit. If it is not, see what the home will do to make it available.

Although it is difficult for the layperson to evaluate the effectiveness of a nursing home's therapy programs, you can at least tour its facilities. The physical therapy area, an important feature in every home, should be equipped with parallel bars and other equipment designed to strengthen muscles and restore coordination. The area for occupational therapy should be well stocked with arts and crafts supplies as well as an array of equipment designed to help disabled residents learn to perform the routine tasks of daily life.

Besides asking how many hours licensed specialists spend in the home, it is equally important to determine how well orderlies and aides reinforce the therapy sessions by helping residents to take walks, comb their hair or dress themselves, or simply by encouraging them to talk. You can ask the administrator if the home trains orderlies and aides to assist with rehabilitation therapy, but you can also make your own observations. Are most of the residents sitting in wheelchairs, or are some walking with the help of aides? Do aides try to encourage residents who have difficulty speaking to communicate with them? A home in which many residents are actively involved in various programs with the help of aides is probably one that has a positive commitment to rehabilitative therapy.

Nursing and Personal Care

The daily comfort and well-being of nursing home residents depends, above all, upon the attitudes of the staff, especially the aides and orderlies who are responsible for so much of their care. Although the administrator, medical director and director of nursing set the policies of their institutions, it is in the activities of the aides and orderlies that you can most clearly see a home's institutional attitudes in action. The following list of an orderly's or aide's duties on a typical morning shift will give you some idea of their responsibilities for resident care.

- Check in promptly at 7 A.M.
- Report to charge nurse for assignments.
- Make rounds with night shift. All residents should be clean and dry with tidy rooms.
- Start morning care: offer bedpan or bathroom assistance; wash face and hands; brush teeth with toothpaste or denture powder and rinse out mouth; prepare for breakfast; roll up bed and put on bib.
- Pass out trays.
- Assist and feed residents.
- Pick up trays; chart intake and output and percentage eaten; return trays to food cart; lower bed.
- Listen to the tape-recorded report from the previous shift, noting special needs of individual residents.
- Offer bedpan or bathroom assistance to residents, cleaning and changing residents as required.
- Continue morning care, with priority given to the sickest and the wettest. Assist with showers. Everyone must be clean and functioning by 11 A.M. Leave rooms and beds until last. Remember always to be concerned about the resident's privacy.
- Take break when quiet time occurs during morning care.
- Shower days: give shampoo at least weekly or as necessary; use a shower cap with women to protect a recent set. Give sponge or bed bath on nonshower days.
- Assist with dressing and grooming, including combing hair, moisturizing dry skin, providing nail care and shaving.
- If directed by doctor's orders, apply or adjust restraints as necessary for the safety and well-being of the resident.
- Check incontinent residents every two hours.
- Every two hours, reposition any resident who cannot do so alone. Massage all pressure areas after turning.
- Make beds, tidy rooms, make certain call lights are within reach; note personal care items that need replacement.
- Assist with bedpan or bathroom needs.
- Lunch break.

- Pass out trays; feed, if necessary, and chart percentage eaten.
- Incontinent rounds at 1 P.M.
- Touch up rooms.
- Assist residents to bed as necessary for naps; cover with blankets.
- Get residents up and active.
- Complete special assignments.
- Before 2 P.M., chart vital signs (blood pressure, temperature, pulse and respiration); I&O's (fluid intake and urine output); S&A's (sugar and acetone); and B.M. (bowel movement).
- Incontinent rounds at 3 P.M.
- Give information to charge nurse for her report to the oncoming shift.
- Pour fresh ice water for all residents.
- Make rounds with incoming shift.
- Check out at 3:30 P.M.

As you observe the aides and orderlies, you should bear in mind that these are not well-paid professionals but workers who perform the physically and emotionally exhausting labor of caring for the elderly with little or no formal training and for very low wages. Simply attending to the basic bodily needs of so many incapacitated and often incontinent patients keeps them hard at work for most of their shifts. Considering these circumstances, you may well be surprised to see how many of these attendants perform their duties with a friendly, caring attitude. If you find a home in which attendants are neat and well groomed, attentive to the residents' needs, and pleasant and gentle in their ministrations, you will have a good preliminary indication of quality care.

Although you may wish to inquire about the ratio of aides and orderlies to residents in each of the homes you visit, you can expect to find little variation in these numbers, which are mandated by law in most states (usually at about three staff hours per resident per day). If state inspectors find a home operating below the specified ratio, their report will cite this as a violation. Another way to judge whether a nursing home is actually understaffed is to ask how many privately paid aides or nurses are on duty at the time. Some homes routinely ask residents to hire special help to compensate for their own staffing deficiencies. If many residents are paying for the services of private aides and orderlies, this could be a sign that a nursing home is not delivering the services it promises.

The appearance of the residents will also give you a great deal of information about the kind of care a home provides. All the residents should look clean, well groomed and comfortable. Everyone should have freshly shampooed hair, neatly trimmed fingernails and clean clothing. Men's beards should be freshly shaved or nicely trimmed. Incontinent patients should be kept dry and odor-free.

Beyond well-groomed residents, however, there should be clearly noticeable efforts on the staff's part to encourage residents to be active and to participate in the social setting of the home.

According to the *Code of Federal Regulations* (see Bibliography), the goal of any good nursing home should be to restore or improve, if possible, but at least to maintain the residents' psychological, social and physical condition. Keep that in mind as you observe the staff members' interactions with residents. An elderly woman who is struggling for five minutes to retie a shoelace is not necessarily being neglected. Residents should be encouraged to do things for themselves. Staff members should be watchful, caring and supportive of their efforts and should treat the residents with dignity and respect at all times.

Personal appearance is as important to the elderly as to anyone else. Nursing home residents should be encouraged to wear their own street clothes, if possible, to help them retain a sense of their own identities. A woman who has been accustomed to regular visits to a beauty shop would be devastated at the thought of not being able to maintain her appearance. Does the home have a beauty shop or a visiting hairstylist? Do the aides help women use shower caps to protect their hair? Does the home have a barbershop or visiting barber for the men? Are residents allowed to use their own electric shavers? If not, who shaves the men? A home that encourages residents to take pride in their appearance is likely to be one that nurtures self-esteem in other ways as well.

Food Preparation and Service

Meals are major events in the daily lives of most nursing home residents. Although the first concern of a good nursing home is to provide for the individual nutritional needs of the residents, many of whom are on special diets, meals and snacks should also be tasty and varied enough to make them appealing. Food service should be attractive and pleasant enough to make mealtime an enjoyable experience for the residents.

Even if your first visit to a nursing home does not take place at mealtime, you can still take some steps to assess the quality of food service. You may not be permitted to tour the home's kitchen, because the laws of most states restrict access to authorized personnel and state inspectors. But you can ask to see the printed menus for several weeks and try to judge their attractiveness and variety as well as their nutritional balance. After looking at the menus, you may want to ask some additional questions. Are the fruits and vegetables they serve generally fresh, canned or frozen? Are substitutes available for foods a resident dislikes? Does the home have a policy of providing vitamin and mineral supplements to residents?

Especially if your relative has special dietary requirements, you may wish to speak with the dietician or food supervisor to determine how these needs will be met. (Although most states require a licensed dietician to supervise menu planning, few homes employ full-time dieticians.) Even if your relative is able to eat a normal diet now, the time may come when he or she will require special food preparation. A good home should be able to provide any special diet a physician prescribes, including mechanically ground and puréed food.

The best way to judge the quality of dietary service is to visit a home during mealtime. You can tell a great deal about how well the food is prepared simply by seeing what a typical meal looks like. Don't be put off if the food is served on thin plastic or paper plates. Although china is more attractive, the cheaper and far more sanitary disposable dishes are being used in most homes these days. Since mealtime is the highlight of the day for many people, it is the author's personal feeling that the meals should be served in the most attractive way possible.

The quality of the mealtime experience also depends on how the food is served, both in the dining room and in residents' rooms. Are meals served at the proper temperature and under sanitary conditions? Are residents given enough time to finish eating without feeling rushed? How do the orderlies and aides treat the residents who cannot feed themselves? Some homes allow as much as a two-hour period for meals in order to give each resident who needs help the undivided attention of a staff member. In other homes with shorter mealtimes, a single staff member may be responsible for feeding as many as four helpless residents at once.

While you are visiting a home, you can take the opportunity to ask a sampling of residents how they enjoy their meals. While you should not be surprised to hear some individual grumbling, as you would in any school or other institutional setting, you should be able to get some sense of the general level of satisfaction by talking with a number of people. This informal survey is well worth the time it takes because the quality of food service tends to be a good general indication of the quality of care in a nursing home.

Social Services

Adjusting to the restrictive regimen of life in a nursing home is a painful process for many elderly people. A good counseling program can help to ease the transition and ensure that a resident's emotional and social needs will not go unrecognized.

Although federal law mandates that skilled nursing facilities must provide adequate social services for their residents, the actual availability as well as the quality of these services varies greatly from one home to another. A large, well-run facility may employ one or more full-time professional social workers to counsel residents who are experiencing emotional or psychological problems. A smaller home may have a part-time professional on its staff or perhaps a layperson who serves in this capacity under the supervision of a consulting professional. If a home provides no social services on the premises, it should at least have an ongoing arrangement for referring residents to social service agencies in the community.

Some homes with well-staffed social services departments have a social worker who meets with prospective residents and their families to help them explore the appropriateness of nursing home placement for the older person. In others, a counseling session involving both the new resident and her or his family is an important part of the admissions process.

A nursing home with an active, well-staffed social services program is likely to be one that is strongly committed to caring for the emotional as well as the physical needs of the residents. Unless you meet with a home's social worker as part of the preadmission procedure, it will be difficult for you to evaluate the quality of its social services. By inquiring into the qualifications of the social workers and the number of hours per week they work with the residents, you will at least have some indication of the availability of these services.

Recreational Activities

A varied schedule of recreational activities enhances the quality of life in a nursing home. A good activities program provides welcome breaks in the residents' daily routine and offers enough diversity to let elderly people choose how they will spend their leisure time. Recognizing the importance of recreational programs in nursing homes, most states require that a home employ one activities director for every hundred residents.

The best way to evaluate the activities programs of the nursing homes you visit is to ask to see the recreational calendars for several different weeks. It should include a variety of choices, encompassing both active and passive forms of entertainment—from sports, dances, games and discussion groups to movies and live entertainment. A full calendar that includes occasional trips outside the nursing home and visits from community groups makes residents feel more in touch with the outside world.

Because a nursing home has the obligation to provide for the residents' spiritual needs, regularly scheduled religious services should be part of every home's calendar of events. If the church or synagogue has been an important part of your older relative's life, you should make certain that he or she will be comfortable with the forms of worship the home provides.

A well-run nursing home will provide many more activities than those formally scheduled on their calendar. Bedridden and mentally disoriented patients should also be provided with frequent recreational activities on an individual basis. Even if your relative is ambulatory and alert, it would be a good idea to ask your tour guide what activities the home offers its bedridden and senile residents. The response will give you another indication of the quality of care the home provides.

In many nursing homes, volunteers help to create lively, varied activities programs. Their participation in this and other areas of nursing home life helps to diminish the isolation of the residents and makes them feel that they have not been forgotten. Whether or not you and your family are interested in doing volunteer work in the home in which your relative lives, it is worth inquiring about each home's volunteer program. A large and active contingent of volunteers indicates that the home is open to the scrutiny of outsiders and that it recognizes the value of making its residents feel that they are still part of the community.

Costs Not Covered by Daily Rate

Even if you have already checked the daily rates of each of the homes you visit, you should have a detailed discussion of financial matters with the administrators of each of the homes you are considering seriously, in order to avoid unpleasant surprises in the future. In addition to the daily rates, which can vary considerably from one institution to another, a number of other factors can make the actual cost of residents' care much higher than the basic per diem charges.

The daily rate should cover the cost of basic services a home provides: room and board, nursing and personal care services and recreational activities. Some nursing homes charge additional fees for equipment, supplies and services that others provide without resident contributions. Equipment such as wheelchairs and walkers may be subject to a rental fee. Some homes even require that residents purchase these items from them. Residents may incur additional charges for supplies such as dressings, catheters, adult diapers, lotions, rubber gloves and even tissues and disposable towels. Some homes bill residents for services that would seem to be routine: visits by the house physician, physical therapy sessions and nursing services such as changing dressings or administering enemas. Prescriptions are always an additional cost unless the resident is receiving

Medicaid. In homes that require that all prescriptions and supplies be purchased from their own pharmacy, these costs may be significantly higher than usual.

Because these costs can add up to a considerable monthly sum, you should ascertain exactly which services are covered by the daily rate and which are extra. The administrator or the billing office should be willing to furnish you with a list of supplies and services that are billed separately and their actual cost. When you add a monthly estimate of these extra costs to the per diem charges of each home you are considering, you may well find that their actual comparative costs are far different from what their daily rates led you to believe.

Another cost that varies widely from one home to another is the rate charged for holding a bed for a resident who has to be hospitalized for a brief period. Many homes charge the full daily rate to hold an empty bed until a resident's return while others charge a reduced rate for a short period of time. Medicare and Medicaid have only minimal coverage for holding costs. Because moving a frail, elderly person to a new home after a hospital stay is so traumatic, many residents and their families will pay these costs, however high they are, to ensure continuity of care. To prepare for this possibility, you should inquire about the holding costs of each home you are considering.

It is also a good idea to ask each administrator for a precise estimate of the costs of services your relative will require that are *not* currently covered by Medicare or Medicaid.

The other major factor that may have a critical effect on the cost of nursing home care is future cost increases. At one time most institutions set limits on their future annual rate increases, but in recent years the inflation rate has become so unpredictable that administrators are no longer willing to operate with restrictions of this kind. Since you are unlikely to find a home that offers a guaranteed limit on future rate increases, the best you can do is to inquire about each home's recent history of increases and their projection of costs in the near future.

Contracts

While you are speaking with the administrator, you should also ask to see a sample copy of the home's standard contract. It is wise to have an attorney review this document carefully to make sure it covers all the contingencies that are likely to arise in the course of a relationship that may last for a number of years.

Although nursing home contracts, like most contractual agreements, can take a variety of forms, every contract should clearly spell out the rights, duties and obligations of both the institution and the resident. The contract should state the services and provisions offered by the home, the arrangements for regular, consultative and emergency medical services, and the rate and terms of payment. A good contract will clearly indicate which services are included in the per diem rate and which entail additional charges.

If you are considering a home that requires life care contracts, you should definitely arrange for a lawyer to review the contract carefully before you make your final decision. Under contracts of this kind, the residents convey all or some portion of their assets to the nursing home in exchange for the home's commitment to take care of them for the rest of their lives. Life care contracts, which are prohibited in several states, including New York, and tightly regulated in others, must be approached with special caution.

The primary disadvantage of life care contracts is that they require residents to give up in advance the ultimate economic bargaining power they might otherwise have—the freedom to take their business elsewhere if they are dissatisfied with the service they receive. Since the home receives the entire lifetime payment at the time the resident arrives, the institution has no economic incentive to continue providing quality service. If the home becomes insolvent or loses its license, the resident could be left penniless and without legal recourse. And unless the contract clearly indicates to the contrary, a home can take the position that "lifetime care" includes only routine nursing care and not the services required to meet acute medical needs.

The strongest appeal of these life care contracts is that they appear to provide total future security. For an older person who faces a protracted illness with limited assets and questionable eligibility for Medicare or Medicaid, this may seem to be an ideal arrangement; but a life care contract is always a gamble of sorts. If a resident dies shortly after his or her property is transferred to the home, the institution's profits will vastly exceed the minimal cost of care. Many life care facilities are excellent institutions that provide their residents with comprehensive quality care, but a life care contract in the hands of an unscrupulous administrator can be dangerous. No one should sign such a contract without carefully investigating the financial stability of the home and the reputations of its board members and administrators and seeking the best legal advice you can find.

NURSING HOME EVALUATION CHECKLIST

This checklist will help you organize your investigations. If you review the questions in advance, you will be able to answer many of them yourself, simply by knowing what to look for as you tour each home. Others will require answers from administrators or other staff members.

I. *Licenses, Accreditations and Inspection Reports*

    A. Current state nursing home license?
    B. Current license for nursing home administrator?
    C. Certified for federal Medicaid and Medicare programs?

   D. Accredited by the American Health Care Association's Quest for Quality Program?

   E. Violations cited on state inspector's report?

II. *Location*

   A. Pleasing to the resident?

   B. Convenient for visiting?

   C. Readily accessible to resident's personal physician?

   D. Close to a hospital?

   E. Safe for ambulatory residents?

III. *Physical Accommodations*

   A. Grounds

      1. Is there an outdoor garden or terrace with benches?

      2. Do ambulatory residents use these outdoor spaces on nice days?

      3. Are there ramps to allow handicapped residents access to the grounds?

   B. General impressions of the physical plant

      1. Is it scrupulously clean and odor-free?

      2. Does the atmosphere seem comfortable and welcoming?

      3. Are lounges and other public areas attractive, cheerful and comfortably furnished?

      4. Are lounges and recreation rooms being used by the residents?

   C. Bedrooms

      1. Is the space adequate?

         a. Easy access to each bed?

         b. Room for wheelchairs to maneuver?

         c. No more than four beds to a room?

2. Is the furniture comfortable and appropriate?
   a. A comfortable chair for each resident?
   b. Reading lights?
   c. Adequate drawer and closet space?
   d. Draperies for each bed for privacy?
   e. Nurse call bell by each bed?
3. Are residents allowed to bring personal belongings to give their rooms individuality?

D. Bathroom facilities
1. Convenient to bedrooms?
2. Easily accessible to residents in wheelchairs?
3. Equipped with hand grips and nurse call bells?
4. Nonskid surfaces in bathtubs and showers?

E. Safety features
1. Accident prevention
   a. Well lighted throughout?
   b. Safe and convenient for residents who have difficulty walking?
      1) Handrails in hallways and grab bars in bathrooms?
      2) Hallways wide enough for two wheelchairs to pass easily?
      3) No obstructions or hazards underfoot?
   c. Sturdy furniture that cannot easily be tipped?
2. Fire safety
   a. Does the home meet federal and state codes? (You can ask to see the latest inspection report.)
   b. Is there a written emergency evacuation plan?
   c. Are frequent fire drills conducted?
   d. Are exits clearly marked, unobstructed and readily opened from the inside?
   e. Are stairways enclosed and stairway doors kept closed?

IV. *Medical Care*

A. Does the home have a medical director? If so, who?

B. Will the resident be able to continue being treated by his or her own personal physician after entering the home?

C. What provisions will the home make for specialized medical services the resident may need now or in the future?

D. Is a physician available to provide emergency care?

E. Will the resident receive a thorough physical examination immediately before or at the time she or he is admitted to the home?

F. Does the home keep good medical records, including detailed plans for patient care?

G. Is there any effort to involve the resident in developing a plan for his care?

H. Can the resident's family purchase his or her medications outside the home?

I. What arrangement does the home have for transferring residents to a hospital if and when this becomes necessary?

V. *Rehabilitation Therapy*

A. Does the home have qualified therapists on its staff in the areas of the residents' needs? If not, what provisions can be made for delivering the prescribed therapy to the resident?
  1. Physical therapy
  2. Occupational therapy
  3. Speech therapy

B. Is the physical therapy room well equipped?

C. Is the occupational therapy room well stocked with equipment and supplies?

D. Do these rooms seem to be heavily used by residents?

E. Are aides and orderlies trained to reinforce the residents' rehabilitation therapy?

F. Do attendants seem to be encouraging disabled residents to practice walking, talking and relearning how to care for themselves?

VI. *Nursing and Personal Care*

A. Is the director of nursing a registered nurse?

B. Is a registered nurse on duty at all times?

C. Does the home have a training program for aides and orderlies?

D. What seems to be the prevalent attitude toward resident care?

    1. Are residents clean and well groomed?

    2. Are many of them wearing street clothes?

    3. Are they encouraged to help themselves whenever possible?

    4. Do most of the residents seem reasonably alert and active?

    5. Are the attendants gentle, cheerful and pleasant?

    6. Do attendants treat residents with dignity and respect?

VII. *Food Preparation and Service*

A. Are the weekly menus appealing?

    1. Do the meals served match the posted menus?

    2. Can residents receive substitutes for foods they dislike?

B. Are meals and snacks served on a reasonable daily schedule?

C. Can the home provide whatever special diet the resident may need?

D. Are visitors allowed to inspect the kitchen? (A negative answer could be because state law prohibits it.)

1. Are food preparation, dishwashing and garbage areas separated?
2. Are kitchen workers observing sanitary food-handling practices?
3. Are all foods that need refrigeration properly stored?

E. Is the dining room attractive and inviting?
   1. Is the furniture comfortable?
   2. Are the tables accessible to residents in wheelchairs?
   3. Is there enough space for wheelchairs to move around?
   4. Are the residents encouraged to come to the dining room if at all possible?

F. Is the food attractively presented? Does it look tasty?

G. How good is the food service to bedridden residents?
   1. Are the meals served at the proper temperature and under sanitary conditions?
   2. Are residents given enough time to finish their meals without feeling rushed?
   3. How well do attendants deal with residents who cannot feed themselves?

VIII. *Social Services*

A. Does a professional social worker participate in the preadmission interviews?

B. Is a professional social worker available to help ease the adjustment of a new resident and his or her family and to deal with other personal problems as they arise?

C. Do treatment plans take into consideration the resident's social and psychological needs?

IX. *Activities Program*

A. How many activities directors does the home employ?

B. Are the weekly schedules of events varied and stimulating?

C. Does the calendar of events include occasional trips away from the home?

D. Does the home have a well-equipped activities room?

E. Are individual as well as group activities available?

F. Are special activities provided for bedridden and senile residents?

G. Are residents encouraged to participate in the activities of their choice but not forced to take part in any that do not appeal to them?

H. Do residents seem to use the activities room and enjoy the recreational program?

I. Does the schedule of activities regularly bring a range of people from the community into the home?

J. Does the home have an active volunteer program?

X. *Religious Observances*

A. Does the home have regular religious services?

B. If so, of what denomination(s)?

C. Is participation voluntary?

D. Can arrangements be made for the residents to continue their own religious observances and receive private visits from their own clergymen or rabbis?

XI. *Residents' Rights and Privileges*

A. Medical
 1. May residents participate in treatment plans and decisions?
 2. Are medical records kept confidential?
 3. Do residents have the right to veto experimental research?

B. Political
 1. Does the home have an active and effective residents' council?

72

    2. Does it have an organization for family members?

    3. Does the home encourage residents to vote in local, state and national elections?

C. Personal

    1. Do residents have freedom and privacy to attend to personal needs?

    2. Is space available for private visits with spouses, lawyers, clergymen, friends and family members?

    3. Can a couple share a room?

    4. Will the home allow residents to bring with them the personal belongings that are most important to them? What about plants? Pets?

    5. How does the home respond to a resident's dissatisfaction with a roommate or tablemate? Are efforts made to accommodate the resident's wishes in matters such as these?

XII. *Financial Considerations*

A. Costs

    1. What is the daily rate?

    2. What services, equipment and supplies are billed as extra charges?

    3. What is the cost of holding a bed during a resident's brief stay in a hospital?

    4. Is a rate increase planned for the near future?

B. Reimbursement under government programs

    1. Is the home certified to participate in Medicare and Medicaid programs?

    2. Will the home accept payment under these programs?

    3. Will the home accept Medicaid payments in the future, even if the resident enters as a private patient?

MAKING THE FINAL CHOICE

After you and the prospective resident have conducted your own investigations of the most suitable nursing homes in a selected area, you will be ready to make an informed choice. Probably no home you visit will strike you as ideal in every way, so you must decide which one best meets the greatest number of criteria you have established.

It is obvious that no home can replace what your relative is leaving behind. All you can realistically expect from the nursing home is for it to meet its contractual obligations, but when it comes to the emotional well-being of your relative, you and the future resident are the experts. And once you have made the best choice together, no matter how well your relative is cared for in the nursing home, it is the kind of attention and support received continually from family and friends that will crucially affect the quality of his or her life there.

4

Easing the Transition

Once you and your relative have decided on the best nursing home, there will be many practical problems to confront, from dealing with the older person's domestic and business affairs to choosing the belongings she or he will take to the home. But don't let activity distract you from pressing *emotional* needs during this critical time.

Mrs. Douglas's family, for example, made that mistake, and she never really recovered from it. As she was lying in the hospital after a stroke that left her partially paralyzed, her son and daughter-in-law, following the advice of her physician, were frantically trying to arrange nursing home placement in time for her discharge. But they were terrified to tell her so, for fear the news would be so upsetting that she would lose her will to live. Whenever she asked what would happen to her, they comforted her with vague assurances that everything would be fine, and she would be able to go home soon. When the time came for her to leave the hospital, they told her they were taking her to a nice place in the country where she could recover for a week or so, until she was stronger. Although her ordeal had left her weak and a bit confused, Mrs. Douglas realized she'd been tricked the moment they drove up to the nursing home, and she began crying hysterically. Her son and daughter-in-law checked her in hurriedly and fled as soon as possible, unable to deal with her pain. They decided to give her a few weeks to "adjust" before they went back to visit her.

Mrs. Douglas spent those lonely days in the home, first weeping and then screaming with rage. Alarmed by her agitated state, the staff nurse contacted her physician, who prescribed sedatives to keep her calm. By the time her family finally came to visit, Mrs. Douglas was so lethargic and withdrawn that she barely seemed to notice their presence. "This is just what I was afraid of," her son said as they were leaving, never realizing that he had made his fear a self-fulfilling prophecy. If he had been able to help his mother understand and gradually accept the need for nursing home placement, she would at least have had a chance to make a comfortable adjustment.

Of course, no one's first choice would be to enter a nursing home. Faced with the necessity, however, most older people can accept it and make the best of it if they are given the practical help and emotional support they need to make the transition. But they do need time to get used to new ideas and to prepare themselves for new situations.

PREPARING TO ENTER THE HOME

How much traumatic change can an infirm older person bear? That is a very painful question that understandably looms large. But as the case of Mrs. Douglas illustrates, avoiding what must be said can have terrifying results, and, ultimately, anything but the truth will only impede your relative's adjustment. If the full brunt of the truth seems too much to bear for everyone involved, however, partial truths like "We'll just have to see what next month brings" are certainly less damaging than lying, building false hopes or falling into a conspiracy of silence.

The benefit of involving older people—if at all possible—in the decisions that determine their welfare has already been discussed. Surely there could not be a more significant occasion for your relative's participation in decisions than at this critical juncture. Besides feeling the assurance that comes with having a hand in matters, your relative's active role in planning the move to a nursing home allows him or her time to adjust to the idea before being confronted with what might otherwise be an overwhelmingly harsh reality.

You should visit the home together at least once before admission day. (Even those who are severely disoriented or aphasic can benefit from such a visit.) Encourage the voicing of questions, concerns and fears. Open discussions will probably reveal specific apprehensions: Will I be able to smoke, have wine with dinner, see my favorite television programs, etc.? Perhaps the greatest fear is of having to cope with a senile roommate, or of never being able to go outdoors. You may be able to allay many of these fears in advance simply by relating what you have already observed, or by discussing the issues with the nursing home staff. If you cannot determine that these apprehensions are groundless, then honesty and reassurance that you share those concerns will offer the most support. If your relative has had a sudden illness or is injured, leaving little time for discussions at home, apprehensions and discontent can still be dealt with after entering the nursing home. If a stroke or coma makes reciprocal communication impossible, then you at least can speak of the plans you've made. The respect and love that you feel may still come across.

If the older person is admitted to the home in a crisis, be sure to let some time go by before you take any major actions to settle domestic and business affairs. Too many nursing home residents recover from grave illnesses only to discover that their families, assuming the worst, have already disposed of their homes and their possessions. No matter how grim the prognosis appears at first, be sure not to make any irrevocable decisions under pressure. And if your relative regains lucidity, even if nursing home care is still needed, restore control of personal and financial affairs as soon as possible. Everything you can do to encourage independence will improve morale and strengthen the will to live.

Assuming that your relative's admission is to be a less stressful one, call the home's business office a few days before checking in to make sure everything is in order. Make certain all necessary applications have been properly filed and that you know when payments are to be made (usually in advance, and penalty charges may be assessed). If you expect Medicare, Medicaid, or private insurance to cover all or part of the nursing home bill, be sure that they have the necessary documentation completed to handle the claims.

State laws require that a written admission agreement must be completed before a new resident enters a nursing home. This agreement is in effect a contract, and, as mentioned earlier (see Contracts, p. 65), it should state the services and provisions offered by the home. It should also state the nursing home's policy with regard to refunds in the event the resident leaves the home. Any funds or property to be held for safekeeping for the resident by the home should also be listed in the admissions agreement. Prior to admission, most homes will also require written instructions for funeral arrangements. Remember that this admission agreement is a legal and binding contract. Read it carefully and make sure you understand it thoroughly.

State laws also require that the new resident receive a thorough physical examination before entering a nursing home or immediately upon admission. Be sure to arrange for this examination, either by the older person's physician or by the nursing home's staff physician, before admission day. Also check to be sure that your relative's personal physician has forwarded complete medical records, along with prescriptions for the medications required. You should be aware that the nursing home will not allow you to bring nonprescription medications for the older person. In many states, homes also prohibit new residents from bringing with them supplies of prescribed medications that have been opened, unless they came from a hospital pharmacy.

In addition to taking care of these standard arrangements with the business office, you can help ensure a more comfortable transition for the prospective resident by communicating with other members of the nursing home staff beforehand. The more you can learn about the home, its services and its accommodations, the better you can help prepare your relative for it. For instance, before discussing what belongings to take to the nursing home, see how much space will be available. Ask any questions, large or small, that you know are troubling the older person.

Just as the nursing home staff can help you prepare your relative for life in the new home, you can greatly assist staff members by sharing pertinent personal facts about the new resident. The most effective way to accomplish this is to write down, in an organized fashion, everything you know about the older person's present physical and mental state, diet, daily routine, personal habits, tastes and interests. Encourage your relative to help you with this task. This profile will be particularly useful if he or she is to share a room. In any event, a well-informed staff can be effective in helping the new resident make a comfortable adjustment to life in the home.

WHAT TO TAKE

Leaving behind a lifetime's accumulation of cherished possessions is one of the most painful emotional adjustments confronting any older person preparing to enter a nursing home. A private room in the most luxurious home offers a resident very little space for personal belongings; the more common double or triple rooms provide even less. You can ease the trauma of the move by helping your relative make a realistic choice of the few possessions that will be most useful and meaningful. Even if the older person will enter the nursing home from a hospital, she or he should be given an active voice in this decision.

Clothing and Other Necessities

The clothing that a new resident should take to the home depends on his or her physical condition and your laundry arrangements. A resident must have at least enough outer garments, underwear and bathrobes to last from one laundry day to the next—generally a one-week interval if the nursing home is laundering your relative's clothes. (If you launder them yourself, a large plastic pail with a cover and a supply of plastic liners for dirty laundry is helpful.)

Those residents who can move around freely can usually bring the same indoor and outdoor clothing they were accustomed to wearing at home. If the resident's laundry will be done by the nursing home, however, the clothes should be made of fabrics that can withstand high-temperature washing. Each resident should also have at least two warm, washable robes to wear between the resident's room and the bathroom. Most homes will furnish nightgowns, but residents may use their own if they conform to their personal care needs. Beyond these minimal requirements, residents may bring whatever clothes they like, bearing in mind the limited amount of closet and drawer space the home will provide.

Incontinent residents will need considerably more sets of clothing. Nonambulatory residents will need fewer dresses, pants and shoes, but they should bring with them two washable lap robes for modesty and warmth. If your relative has limited mobility and has difficulty getting dressed, clothing should be chosen with these special needs in mind. Wheelchair-bound residents need warmer clothes than those who can move around freely and should be well supplied with loose-fitting cardigan sweaters or shawls. All clothing should be selected to make dressing as easy as possible.

Nursing home aides find it easier to care for nonambulatory women if their dresses are slit up the backs and fastened with a few ties or pieces of Velcro. Unfortunately, some homes will simply alter a new resident's clothing without forewarning her family. This is the kind of painful shock that can make entering a nursing home unnecessarily traumatic for new residents and everyone who cares about them. If your relative cannot easily dress herself, you should ask whether the home will require that her clothes be altered. If so, it will be far better to explain this in advance or even do it yourself than to risk the helplessness and panic that will naturally result when she suddenly discovers that strangers have ''ruined'' all her clothes.

The list of personal care items the new resident should take depends, in part, on the home. Some nursing homes provide soap, toothbrushes and toothpaste, shampoo, facial tissues and other necessities at no additional charge; others charge inflated prices for them. Residents are generally expected to bring their own brushes and combs, shaving equipment, deodorant and other personal care items. Take only a small supply of soap, tissues and other necessities and replenish them when necessary. Larger quantities will be difficult to store and could even be stolen.

You should also include other personal care products the new resident has been accustomed to using. A favorite perfume, after-shave or scented body lotion can help provide a sense of continuity, even for mentally disoriented residents. A nursing home is not a hospital but a home, and residents should be provided with all the products they need to maintain self-esteem.

Other Personal Belongings

The number of personal possessions permitted will vary from one nursing home to another. In some, generally the older ones, a resident may be able to have a favorite chair, pictures on the wall and other familiar objects. In many newer ones, personal touches are limited to a few small items. Well before moving day, check carefully with the home to determine the kinds of possessions allowed. To prevent lassitude and disorientation, every effort should be made to provide the new resident with whatever gives comfort and pleasure. Here are some suggested items that might help your relative feel more comfortable:

Photographs, a favorite painting, pillow or afghan; a good reading lamp in a convenient position and a frequently changed supply of books and magazines; a radio with cassette player for recorded books, music, messages from friends, etc.; a portable television set with video cassette recorder and earphones for additional freedom; and a clock and calendar with easy-to-read numbers.

Valuables

Whether the new resident should take valuable jewelry or other possessions to the nursing home presents a particularly difficult choice, both for the older person and the family. Theft is an all too common problem in nursing homes today, and even the finest homes do not guarantee the safety of residents' valuable possessions. When you also consider the equally strong possibility that jewelry may be misplaced by absentminded older people or harried aides, prudence clearly dictates that all the new resident's valuables should be locked up in a safe deposit box on admission day.

If your relative is mentally alert, this is an issue that should be thoroughly discussed before admission day. The risk of losing the new resident's valuables should be weighed against the emotional costs of protecting them. Older people entering nursing homes have already suffered, and will continue to suffer, so many losses that you may feel loath to inflict yet another one by depriving a loved one of his or her most cherished possessions. Your mother may feel bereft without the diamond engagement ring she has worn for fifty years or the earrings she inherited from her grandmother. Even worse, she may blame you for "stealing" them from her. In a situation like this, it may well be worth the risk of loss to allow older people the comfort of keeping the valuables that mean so much to them.

Labeling and Recording Personal Belongings

Every article of clothing and every personal care item the resident takes to the nursing home should be labeled. The resident's name should be printed in all clothing with an indelible laundry marker, and personal care items should be marked with name or room number. Be sure to label eyeglasses so that they don't end up being worn by another resident, and make sure you have the lens prescription in case of breakage or loss.

Before admission day, you should also make a complete list of all the belongings the older person will be bringing to the home. This list will be most useful if you briefly describe each article individually. A missing "blue and white checked cotton shirt" will be far easier to trace than one of six undescribed shirts. Keep a copy of this list for yourself and take another with you to the nursing home, where it should be recorded during the admission process. Even though nursing homes assume no legal responsibility for loss of or damage to any personal effects, this record will help the staff keep track of the resident's belongings. In addition to articles of clothing and valuables, be sure to note items like eyeglasses, dentures or hearing aids, which can easily be lost or misplaced. If the resident is bringing a wheelchair, gerichair or walker, it should be registered, with its make and other particulars, and be prominently labeled.

ADMISSION DAY

On the day you are going to check in, a last-minute call is advisable to make sure there is no confusion about dates, check-in time (usually midmorning), etc. The reception you get when you arrive can vary considerably from one home to the next.

Some nursing homes go to great lengths to make a new resident's entrance into the home a pleasant and reassuring experience. A staff member may spend the entire first day with the older person and his or her family, showing them around the home and introducing them to all the details of daily life. A welcoming committee of residents may greet the new arrival. Other homes, which may be excellent in other ways, make little or no special effort to help the newcomer feel at home or adjust to a new environment.

No matter how the nursing home staff customarily greets a new resident, it is crucially important for *you* to be there the entire first day. If possible, drive her or him to the home yourself, or be in the ambulance if one is necessary, so that your relative will not arrive alone. The admission process involves many time-consuming administrative details, as well as unpacking, meeting staff members and introducing the new resident. Since there will be so many things to do, you may want to bring another close friend or relative along with you to stay at the older person's side while you take care of business. The support of the family through this first day will make your relative feel more comfortable and reassured of not being abandoned to the care of strangers.

You are entering a complex, closely knit community that may be your relative's home for some time, and you will be scrutinized very closely by staff members and residents alike. So keep in mind that first impressions are indelible and that news travels quickly in the small world of a nursing home.

Although the procedures of individual homes vary considerably, you can expect a lengthy intake interview, in which the admissions officer or some other staff member will gather a wide range of detailed information about the new resident, from physical condition to hobbies and interests, etc. Unless the older person is totally bedridden, he or she should be with you during this interview and should be encouraged to speak as much as possible. At some point during the day, the new resident may need to undergo a physical examination. You may need to check with the business office to finalize your financial and contractual arrangements and make certain it has all the documentation required. Make certain to file a complete list of the new resident's belongings with the appropriate staff member.

Aside from administrative and medical procedures, you will want to help your relative unpack and get settled in new surroundings: getting to know some of the other residents, keeping him or her company during the first meals, introducing yourselves at the table and greeting the residents as you begin to explore other parts of the home. You can use times when your relative is involved with medical procedures or is resting to converse with other residents. You may be able to help find people who share similar interests and experiences.

When you first introduce yourselves, don't be surprised or alarmed if you don't always receive an immediate reply—and don't assume that everyone who fails to respond to you at first is senile. Many older people find it difficult to cope with new faces or any breaks in their familiar routines. Accepting a new roommate, for instance, can be as traumatic for the established resident as it may be for the new one. Some of the residents may need time before they begin accepting overtures of friendship. With this in mind, be friendly but low key in your first contacts with the other residents. There will be plenty of time in the months to come for interaction with other residents.

During this busy first day, try to talk quietly about first impressions. Shock and exhaustion may prevent communication, but your relative can at least be assured that you want to hear his or her real feelings. When you have to leave, say goodbye as you always do—with your usual handshake, hug or kiss. Try not to be alarmed by the grief the older person is likely to express at this time, even though you feel the same way. Say exactly when you will return and inform the aide on duty that you are leaving, so that she can reassure the new resident in your absence.

THE ADJUSTMENT PERIOD

During the first few months after your loved one enters a nursing home, you may need to offer all the understanding, compassion and hope you can muster. It takes time for any new resident to adjust to the overwhelming changes. While struggling with the disabilities that made nursing home placement necessary, he or she must learn to adapt to a new environment, new faces, new routines. Abruptly deprived of their homes and their freedom, new residents often suffer physical or mental setbacks during the adjustment period. Some older people soon find themselves enjoying the activities and companionship that the home provides. Others go through a longer period of crisis before they finally come to terms with their new lives. New residents may become angry or confused, lethargic or withdrawn, and these emotional reactions may adversely affect their health for a time. Even comatose patients often suffer temporary physical reversals during their first days in a new environment.

Don't panic if your relative's physical or mental state seems to be deteriorating during her or his first weeks or months in the home. Nursing home professionals observe that it can take as long as six months for older people to adapt reasonably well to nursing home life. If you bear in mind that these setbacks are common and usually temporary, you'll be in a better position to help your relative adjust and lead as rich and full a life as possible for the duration of this stay. The next two chapters suggest strategies for enriching the resident's life, making sure he or she receives the best possible care during the adjustment period and in the weeks and months that follow.

The new resident is not the only one who goes through an emotional crisis after entering the home. Placing a relative in a nursing home is always a traumatic experience for the family. Even when the facts clearly indicate that there was no other choice, feelings of guilt and fear, of loss and even anger are understandable. And if the older person reacts adversely to the first weeks in the home, the family will suffer even more.

As you're trying your best to care for the new resident during this difficult time, don't ignore your own emotional needs and those of the rest of your family. If it helps, share your feelings with someone in whom you have confidence. Recognizing that this need exists, some nursing homes provide counseling for families as well as for residents, both before admission and during the adjustment period. Many families of nursing home residents have also formed self-help support groups in recent years. Some are composed of families of residents in a single nursing home; others are based in the community. If such a group does not yet exist in your area, you may want to start one yourself. By finding productive ways to express and work through your emotional responses to this family crisis, you'll be better able to help your relative deal with the adjustment to life in the nursing home.

5

Enriching the Life of the Nursing Home Resident

As stated in Chapter 3, even the best nursing homes with the most outstanding counseling, therapy and activities programs cannot provide their residents with the kinds of stimulation, support and encouragement that comes from loving family members and friends. Without frequent contact with visitors, it's all too common for residents to become apathetic and depressed. Friends and family play a crucial role in improving the mental and physical well-being of nursing home residents by keeping them interested and involved in the world outside the home, sharing memories and interests, and making them feel that their thoughts and feelings are still highly valued.

MAKING THE MOST OF YOUR VISITS

Many people find it difficult to act natural in any institutional setting. When you first see your relative under these unfamiliar circumstances, your empathy may be a serious obstacle.

Unfortunately, some never get beyond this initial discomfort, and their visits consist of nothing but perfunctory exchanges of commonplace information punctuated by long, painful silences. Although visits of this kind are better than none at all, there are ways to make the time you spend in the nursing home a pleasant and enriching experience for everyone concerned.

Nursing Home Etiquette and Attitudes

From the outset, a positive attitude is essential. If you can brighten the days for your relative and other residents, their pleasure will make your visits rewarding. Try to put yourself in the resident's place and ask yourself how you would like to be treated if you were in that situation. Instead of simply dropping by the home whenever it suits you, call and give your relative a choice in deciding when you should come to visit. Encourage the older person to be as assertive as possible in handling personal affairs and small problems within the home. Many families make older people far more helpless than they need to be by insisting on taking too much control of their lives and by treating the elderly with physical disabilities as if they were children. Remember that the weakest bodies can still house lively minds and rich emotional depths, as *That Time of Year: A Chronicle of Life in a Nursing Home,* a moving memoir written by Joyce Horner (poet, novelist and former professor of English), so powerfully attests. There is no better way for an outsider to understand how rich the internal life of an apparently feeble nursing home resident can be than by reading this uplifting book. With patience and understanding, you will be able to find ways to give your relative or friend the reassurance and encouragement needed to live as full a life as possible in the nursing home.

Remember, too, that the other residents are all part of the community that is now the older person's home, and that they are sensitive to your kindness and respect. Make a particular effort to get to know the people who are important to your relative. Many nursing home residents are lonely; more than half have no one to visit them; and one-fourth of them have no family at all. A few friendly words can mean so much. Avoid impersonal and informal terms like "honey" or "dear." Learn as many names as possible, but, as I've already explained, don't be surprised if your first overtures are ignored. Gentle perseverance, however, will probably be acknowledged and appreciated.

Staff members, from the head nurse to the aides, are of fundamental importance to a resident's well-being. The way you treat them can make an enormous difference, positive or negative, in the quality of care your relative receives. (Chapter 6 contains a more detailed discussion of how families can work with staff members to monitor the care of the resident.) Unreasonable demands or impulsive complaints are not well received, so if you see a problem, talk with the aide involved or with the head nurse, if necessary, and try to resolve it in a friendly, helpful way. Above all, show appreciation and respect for the difficult and often unrewarding work these people do.

The great majority of nursing home administrators discourage the common practice of tipping or giving individual gifts to aides and orderlies, but individual cards with personal notes of gratitude or fruit baskets for each shift to share are appropriate ways of remembering staff members at holiday time. In addition, I feel the most effective way of thanking a staff member for excellent care is by sending a letter of praise to the home's administrator.

Communicating with the Resident

As they start losing their vision, hearing and physical mobility, elderly people tend to become isolated and withdrawn. Without frequent stimulation, their world grows smaller and smaller, until they have little left but their aching, unmanageable bodies to occupy their attention. Under these circumstances, it's no

wonder that so many older people become increasingly queru-
lous and self-absorbed. But most of them do enjoy hearing news
of their family and friends—a son or daughter's professional
achievements or a great-grandchild's latest antics, for example.
Instead of commiserating with your mother's aches and pains,
tell her all about your job, your children and grandchildren,
your plans to buy a vacation house or to redecorate the living
room. Bring photos of your garden in springtime, your new car
or pet, your vacation trip, or family members to make her feel a
part of your activities. If you continue to share your life with
her as you did before, you will no doubt find that your most
routine weeks are filled with small events and details that she
will find interesting and entertaining.

Encourage other family members, including teenagers and
small children, to visit their older relative as often as possible.
Many people leave the children at home when they make their
visits, to avoid disturbing the older people or upsetting the little
ones. Both of these reasons are shortsighted. Few things give
nursing home residents greater pleasure than cuddling a baby or
hearing the laughter of a toddler; and children can learn from an
early age to deal with old age as a normal part of human and
family life. It may take some special preparation, and perhaps
some subtle bribery, before young people begin to feel comfortable visiting the nursing home, but the joy it brings makes the
effort worthwhile.

Another way to brighten the life of the nursing home resident
is to help him or her keep in touch with friends, religious
organizations and the community—even if you have to go out of
your way to find out the latest news. Arrange to bring the
resident's friends to the home for regular visits if they have
trouble getting around on their own. Everything you can do to
stimulate your relative through contact with friends and community will diminish the sense of isolation.

Do everything you can to encourage involvement in the
professional, civic and cultural interests and the hobbies he or
she has always enjoyed: books and articles, photographs of

flower shows, favorite cassettes, etc. And take the time to share them. If your relative can no longer read, you can spend part of your visits reading aloud.

Of course, many nursing home residents may understandably lose interest in the professional or civic activities that used to occupy their time once they can no longer participate in them directly. But older people still need to feel useful after society appears to have no further use for them. Family and friends are probably the only ones who can make them feel that they still have important contributions to make. Instead of the usual lighthearted chatter, think of ways you can solicit advice and support. Your mother may enjoy helping you decide which drapery fabric to choose for your living room or which entrée to serve for a dinner party. You may be able to ask your father's advice about the investments you are making or a garage that you are building. Every time you can find an opportunity to ask your relative's advice, you enhance his or her self-esteem.

Don't make the mistake of trying to hide family problems, disappointments and other bad news. A parent or other close relative who has known you for a lifetime will readily sense that something is troubling you and feel even more helpless if you are hiding your problems. If you try to pretend everything is fine, you will deny her or him the opportunity to share your pain and to give you the benefit of wise advice and solace. Many older people have been saved from lethargy and depression by a family crisis that reminded them how much they still had to contribute.

In your concern to keep your relative in touch with the world outside the nursing home, don't forget to share what happens inside the home, even if it is not a preferred topic. There may be nothing but complaints at first or reluctance to burden you with them. The best way to ensure that life in the nursing home will be as comfortable as possible is to establish and maintain a clear channel of communication. Listen carefully, seriously and sympathetically, and do what you can to soothe the unrest.

Your active interest in the daily activities—from new accomplishments in arts and crafts to the progress in physical therapy—will also strengthen the conviction that he or she is still leading a rich, productive life. Include a special friend in some of your family dinners or excursions. Your interest will help the older person find meaning in the present and inspire greater adjustment efforts.

If your relative enjoys dwelling in the past, accept this as a natural part of the aging process. You can spend many happy hours reliving triumphs and tragedies and rediscovering what daily life was like in the old days. Oral historians, recognizing that the memories of older people are an invaluable and irreplaceable resource, are recording their reminiscences by the thousands. By showing a strong interest in hearing about your relative's past, you will enhance her or his self-esteem and learn precious details of your own family history in the process—which, if your relative is willing, can be recorded for other family members. Listening to memories, incidentally, does not mean that you should do so without helping the older person remain firmly anchored in the present.

But what if the resident is mentally disoriented or emotionally unbalanced? What if the results of a stroke prevent talking or even facial gestures? What kind of communication is possible? Is there any point to visiting?

Dealing with Severe Communication Problems

Many older people in nursing homes suffer from confusion and disorientation all or some of the time. The best way to deal, for example, with your grandfather's disorientation, is to try to put him at ease by giving him clues that will help him establish his bearings. If he sometimes has difficulty recognizing you, it's a good idea to begin by introducing yourself: "Hello, Granddad. It's Michael," or "Hi, Papa. Here's Dana, your granddaughter, back from college." You may also want to check that his hearing aid is adjusted properly, that he is wearing the correct glasses and that the sun is not in his eyes. Avoid testing the older person with questions like ''Do you know me?'' or ''Remember me?'' This approach is embarrassing rather than stimulating. Be considerate and patient, and try not to make him feel pressured in any way. Talk normally; he may follow part, if not all, of what you say. If his mind wanders, follow his shift of attention rather than calling attention to his lapse. You are there to give him the comfort and support of your presence, not to get any particular point across.

It takes great reserves of patience and calm to deal with an older person who suffers from delusions or violent mood swings. If your sweet-tempered mother suddenly begins screaming at you, you'll need to swallow hard and remind yourself not to take her attacks personally. In situations like these, a discussion with the resident's physician may help you cope. Once you understand these outbursts as symptoms of an illness, it will be easier for you to deal with them calmly and impersonally, while waiting for the storm to pass.

Perhaps the most heartbreakingly difficult visits are to residents who have lost the power to speak, because of paralysis or coma. But geriatric professionals agree that visitors are just as beneficial to people in these states as they are to more communicative residents. We cannot assume that the inability to move or respond indicates a total lack of awareness. Even if a man paralyzed by a stroke has shown no signs of mental responsiveness for weeks, his eyes may light up when he hears the voice of his favorite granddaughter. Patients in comas seem to sense the comforting presence of a loved one. Whatever the physical condition of the resident, your familiar voice and your reassuring touch still matter. If your relative is in a physical, mental or emotional state that makes your visits particularly difficult, you may want to ask the home's social worker as well as the resident's doctor for more information and advice about how to communicate productively and offer the greatest comfort. Bear in mind that you can also use your time at the home to monitor the quality of care the resident is receiving, as Chapter 6 will discuss in detail.

IMAGINATIVE GIFTS

Cut flowers are the gift most visitors think of taking to a nursing home resident. For the convenience of the older person and the staff, they should be delivered in vases or other containers. Flowers are always welcome because they bring a touch of natural beauty to the older person's life for a few days. Many people also think of bringing candy or special homemade things to eat. Before you do this, check with the nursing staff to be sure the food you bring will not upset a prescribed dietary plan. A sunhat or visor, a new sweater, or a bottle of perfume, moisturizing lotion or other personal care products are useful, practical gifts for nursing home residents.

But when you're thinking about what you can bring, consider more imaginative, enriching gifts that will help relieve the tedium of daily routine. Instead of cut flowers, for instance, bring a live plant, assuming the home permits them. The gift of a plant will give an older person with some mobility the responsibility of caring for it as well as the continuing gratification of watching it grow. Even if your relative was never an avid gardener, a few plants may awaken a new interest.

Since studies have shown that nursing home residents who were given plants to care for showed striking improvements in their mental attitudes, some homes have added "plant therapy" to their programs. Volunteers at the Laguna Honda Hospital in San Francisco recently built a wheelchair-accessible greenhouse and a small petting zoo, to the delight of their 1,200 older residents. Although some nursing homes have excellent activities programs and facilities that keep their residents involved in the outside world, many do not. As a concerned family member, you can't count on the home to completely fulfill your relative's need for entertainment and mental stimulation. And since you are a major link to the world outside the home, it's up to you to keep the older person physically active and mentally stimulated by bringing interesting gifts that will help fill the endless hours that stretch between your visits.

If, for example, you have an aging father who is mentally alert, encourage him to keep up his earlier interests and hobbies and to cultivate new ones. If he can still read, make sure he is well supplied with books, magazines and newspapers. Some public libraries have outreach services that bring books to nursing home residents. The activities directors of some homes make regular trips to libraries on behalf of the residents, and they may be able to assist residents with their selections. In many communities and in many nursing homes, however, the family must provide residents with reading material. Though your father might not be an avid reader, he might enjoy it now with time on his hands. Ask him what kinds of books or magazines he would like. If he has no requests, bring a variety and note what he picks out. In addition to novels and books pertaining to his profession or hobbies, you may want to try an illustrated book on nature, travel or art. Even older people who can't concentrate on reading will enjoy looking at books and magazines with lots of pictures in them. Many residents also like to browse through illustrated catalogues.

Today, fortunately, those whose vision is severely impaired can still have access to the world of books. Large-print books are available at most public libraries. Many have extensive collections, and even smaller libraries will generally have access to larger collections through interlibrary loan services. *The New York Times* publishes a weekly large-print edition; Reader's Digest Services makes available a number of large-print books and periodicals; and large-print Bibles can be obtained from the American Bible Society. With the aid of a high-powered lighted magnifying glass, many older people who thought they could no longer read can still enjoy these large-print books. Public libraries that provide outreach services for the disabled can provide more information about the various reading aids, including machines that translate print into spoken language, that are now available to the visually handicapped.

Perhaps the best news for older people is the enormous increase in "talking books." Recorded on cassettes, they are still quite expensive, and few public libraries can afford to purchase large collections. The Library of Congress has a superb program for distributing recorded books and magazines (as well as Braille books) free of charge to the visually disabled and to those whose physical disabilities prevent them from handling books. These recorded books are generally distributed by mail, through state or regional libraries. Participants can either select their own titles with the help of catalogues, special subject bibliographies and *Talking Book Topics,* a free bimonthly review of new books and services, or instruct the library to select books for them. This federally funded program will also provide machines free of charge for playing discs and cassettes and whatever other equipment qualified participants need to make use of their materials, including headphones, pillowphones for those confined to their beds, amplifiers for the hearing impaired, and devices to help people with limited mobility use the playback machines. Introducing an older person who can no longer read to this wonderful resource may be the most treasured gift you could possibly offer. For more information, contact your local library or write to the National Library Service for the Blind and Physically Handicapped at this address:

Library of Congress
1291 Taylor Street, N.W.
Washington, D.C. 20011

If the older person has an art or a craft that she or he enjoys—and many residents learn new crafts in the nursing homes—he or she will appreciate gifts of supplies or materials not easily obtained in the home. High-quality watercolors or brushes for painting, fine yarns or new patterns for knitting, or "found objects" for collages will encourage the older person to work with greater enthusiasm.

With a little imagination, you may be able to think of a gift that will inspire many pleasant and productive hours on a new project. A photograph album or scrapbook and a box of old family pictures could give a resident months of enjoyment sorting through and arranging the material while reminiscing with family members and friends, old and new. The gift of a handsome journal or tape recorder could encourage the older person to write down or tape descriptions of events from the past for family and friends. Visitors' participation in projects of this kind can add an enjoyable new dimension to the hours they spend at the home. A resident may also enjoy having a guest book for visitors to sign.

While you're thinking about what you can bring to brighten the life of the nursing home resident, don't forget the things that money can't buy. Especially if the resident can't come home for visits, pictures of a new cat, a new car or a redecorated living room as well as recent photos of the family are most welcome. Handmade cards or drawings from grandchildren or great-grandchildren are also a source of enjoyment and pride. To older people who are bedridden, a beautiful autumn leaf, a bluejay feather, a seashell, or a piece of driftwood you found on the beach may bring greater pleasure than the most expensive gift you could buy. Even the mentally disoriented will enjoy the familiar sight, smell and touch of natural objects from the world outside the walls.

SPECIAL OCCASIONS

If your relative or friend is able to leave the nursing home for short periods of time or overnight, take a brief excursion.

Simply having lunch at a restaurant, taking a scenic car ride, or feeding the ducks in a nearby park is a welcome diversion and creates an atmosphere for intimate and relaxed conversation. Trips to museums or zoos, to concerts or plays can be truly memorable experiences for older people, especially if they share them with their families. Your relative may particularly appreciate returning to services at a familiar church or synagogue. And all the time spent with you and other family members in your own homes will undoubtedly be treasured. If you expect your relative to be in the nursing home for a limited period of time, you may also want to plan a visit to his or her own home as a further incentive for recovery.

If notified in advance, nursing homes usually encourage resident outings, as long as the older person's physician approves. Before assuming that your relative's condition will prohibit outings, check with the physician and staff to determine what kinds of excursions might be possible. You may be pleasantly surprised by the response you receive. Today, people in wheelchairs have a growing access to public facilities, including museums, theaters and restaurants. Incontinence does not necessarily preclude outings of various kinds, as long as you have adequate protective supplies with you.

There are other ways to create special occasions. You can arrange to bring a homecooked meal to share, as long as you check dietary requirements with a staff nurse beforehand. For a birthday or other special occasion, you can also stage a more elaborate party for the older person. Here again, be sure to discuss your plans with the staff well in advance. The head nurse will need to arrange food substitutions for residents with diabetes or allergic conditions. She or he and the rest of the staff can also help you organize the party. To avoid hurt feelings, try to include as many residents as possible in your party plans, and think of sharing any leftovers with the residents and staff members instead of taking them home.

KEEPING IN TOUCH WITH DISTANT FRIENDS AND FAMILY

Children, grandchildren and other relatives and friends who live too far away for frequent visits to the nursing home can keep in close contact with the resident by mail and telephone. Phone calls have the advantage of intimacy and immediacy. Letters filled with news and good wishes can be read and reread, and make the nursing home resident look forward to the daily arrival of the mail. The mail can also bring photographs, clippings and artwork from young children. If the resident has a cassette player, greetings can be sent and received on tape.

Friends or relatives who live close by and visit regularly can help the older person maintain close communication with their distant relatives in various ways. If your relative can't read the letters or play the cassettes, you can volunteer to read the mail or play the tapes each time you visit. Time does not always permit even the most caring nurses and aides to perform this important task for the residents. In the daily flurry, mail can also get lost or misplaced. If you buy a message book and ask the nurse or other staff person to note each letter that arrives, you will at least have a record that will help you track down a misplaced letter. Another way you can help the older person stay in touch with distant friends and relatives is to have him or her dictate letters to you. All of these efforts you make can be a source of real happiness to your relative.

VOLUNTEERING

As you spend more time at the nursing home, you will find yourself getting to know some of the other residents. When you realize how many of them don't have the support of loving families and friends, you'll understand how most nursing home residents depend on the kindness of strangers to enhance the quality of their lives. And you may find yourself *wanting* to help other residents as well as your own relative.

In most nursing homes, volunteers contribute in many ways, from passing out trays and feeding those who need assistance to reading aloud, writing letters, bringing books from the library and taking residents to church and on outings. Volunteers also make nursing homes' activities programs more exciting by leading discussions of books or current events, organizing sing-alongs or quilting projects or teaching the residents photography, painting or other skills.

As you get to know the world of the nursing home, you may want to become involved in some of these volunteer activities. Your participation can be as informal as helping to feed another resident at mealtime or as formal as helping to organize a resident counsel. You may also begin by enlisting your friends to contribute some of their time, or by convincing your church, synagogue or community group to establish an outreach program. If you are interested, speak with the home's director of volunteers, who will be delighted to suggest various ways you can help enrich the lives of all the residents.

6

Monitoring the Resident's Care

Mrs. Lane, an independent elderly widow, had been in good health before she entered a nursing home following surgery for a broken hip. She died five months later, a victim of inadvertent neglect by her family as well as by the expensive, handsomely appointed but temporarily understaffed institution she had chosen. Her error, which proved to be fatal, lay in choosing an institution that was near her own home but hundreds of miles away from any of her children, who were too far away to observe her progress and monitor the care she was receiving. Her story is worth recounting in some detail because it so powerfully illustrates how helpless nursing home residents can be without the alert observation and active advocacy of a concerned family or friends.

Mrs. Lane was brought from the hospital to the nursing home by ambulance. She was having trouble coming out from under the effects of anesthesia and was not totally conscious, as often happens. After ten days in bed, she was dressed every afternoon, put into a wheelchair and tied with a restraint belt because she was unable to sit up unaided. This routine was soon discontinued when staff members noticed that she did not enjoy these periods out of bed. For a while, she was given some physical therapy in the form of a daily walk around her room and down the hallway, but this, too, was soon discontinued after the therapist noted on her record, "Patient does not respond to physical therapy." Soon, she never left her bed, not even to go to the bathroom.

In her own home, Mrs. Lane had socialized with friends and spent a great deal of time reading or watching television. In the nursing home, her room had no television set, she was given no books, and her roommate spoke no English. Because she was rarely taken out of her room, Mrs. Lane's social isolation was almost complete, and her mental stimulation was nonexistent.

To make matters worse, beginning with her first week in the home, Mrs. Lane's diet was limited to the puréed food that her physician prescribed for her after an aide had reported that she had some tendency to choke when she was fed. Revolted by the unappetizing food, never encouraged to sit up and feed herself, she grew weaker and weaker from lack of nutrition.

Mrs. Lane's daughter, who kept in touch with the head nurse via periodic phone calls, was told that her mother's recovery from surgery was "somewhat disappointing" but that she was "resting well." When she made a trip to the home six weeks after Mrs. Lane's arrival, the daughter was astonished to see her mother looking so thin and wasted and showing so many signs of mental disorientation, including hallucinations. The administrator assured her that older people often go through "these phases" as they recover from surgery. On her next visit two months later, the daughter found her mother totally unresponsive and weighing less than a hundred pounds. Mrs. Lane died a month later.

A tragedy like this cannot occur if close relatives or friends are on the scene to represent the interests of nursing home residents and to give them the personal attention and emotional support that is essential to their well-being. Close at hand, a caring relative or friend could have ensured early on that Mrs. Lane had books and a television set in her room and requested a change of roommates. At the first signs of apathy or mental disorientation, her physician could have been asked to make certain that she was not being overmedicated. The mental anguish caused by the restraint belt could have been eased by explaining it. Then, an attentive family member could have encouraged her to do without it as soon as possible and made certain that the physician's order for it was revoked the moment she was stronger. A family member could have insisted that she try solid foods at regular intervals and attempt to feed herself without choking. Later on, someone in her family could have taken her for walks to the common rooms and helped her to get to know some of the other residents as well as suggesting, or, if necessary, demanding that the staff actively encourage her to spend more time outside the confines of her room. As her health improved, her life could have been enriched by trips outside the home.

We can imagine an ideal nursing home in which dedicated staff members have the sensitivity, the commitment and the time to recognize and respond to the unarticulated needs of each resident, analyze the sources of their apathy or depression and, above all, inspire them with the will to live and the hope of recovery. In the real world, all this is too much to expect of the overworked, poorly paid aides who provide most of the daily care to nursing home residents and of the equally overtaxed nurses, physical therapists and doctors whose professional services are more intermittent; their concern is inevitably spread unevenly among the many residents of an institution. This is why, even in the best nursing homes, the supportive presence and active involvement of family and friends make an enormous difference in both the quality of life of the residents and the quality of care they receive.

More and more nursing homes are recognizing the invaluable contributions families can make to the well-being of the resident and are encouraging them to participate in planning and monitoring the care received in the home. Whether or not the home where your relative is residing actively fosters this kind of team effort, there are many things you, and only you, can do to ensure that she or he receives the best care the home can offer.

The case of Mrs. Lane shows that you don't need any specialized knowledge or training to improve the care your relative receives in the nursing home. Your intimate knowledge of the resident and your personal concern, coupled with common sense and willingness to speak up on her or his behalf, are all the qualifications you need to become an effective advocate of the older person's interests.

MAKING YOUR OWN OBSERVATIONS

Regular visits to the nursing home are essential, not only for the morale of the resident, but also for ensuring quality care. Of course, even the most dutiful visiting will do nothing to improve the quality of care the resident receives unless you are prepared to investigate and act to correct any actual or potential problems you observe. A daughter who is painfully aware that her father is growing more apathetic and inactive week by week does him no good if she simply goes home and weeps, instead of insisting that the resident's physician and other staff members work with her to discover the cause of the problem and take corrective action. Once you resolve to assume an active role as the resident's advocate, you can make excellent use of your regular visits to monitor the care.

Simply by visiting the home frequently, you will have access to a great deal of information about the resident's condition and the kind of care received. You will immediately notice whether the older person appears clean, well groomed and comfortable. You will also be aware of any striking changes in physical strength, mental capacity or emotional state. And, in the normal course of a visit, the older person may tell you many things—positive, negative or neutral—about daily life in the home.

During your frank conversations, check on the resident's participation in occupational therapy and other activities; listen for complaints of theft, mistreatment, discomfort, etc. Then, as his or her representative, you will naturally want to verify any complaints expressed and work to correct the situation. But avoid hasty accusations until you have carefully investigated the facts, which may be quite different from the older person's perceptions.

If your relative is aphasic or mentally disoriented, you will need to develop different strategies for finding out about the care he or she is receiving in your absence. In these situations, an alert, talkative roommate can sometimes prove to be a good source of information.

But whether or not you can rely on the resident, it's advisable to vary the times and days of your visits so that you can observe different parts of the daily routine for yourself. If you always visit on Sunday afternoons, for instance, you may find out too late, if ever, that your relative has not been receiving the kind of rehabilitative therapy prescribed.

By dropping in at mealtime, you can see whether your relative is eating well and is being fed properly if assistance is needed. Occasional visits on weekday afternoons will tell you if he or she is clean, well groomed, dressed and taken out of bed every day, not just on visiting days.

By going to the home at different times, you will also get to know more of the aides and orderlies who perform most of the daily tasks. Because they are the ones who feed the residents who need help, they are in the best position to tell you how well your relative is eating. Since they are the ones who actually get the residents out of bed, help them to dress, take them for walks or put them in a wheelchair, they also know a great deal about their daily activity level, their emotional state and their willingness to perform the routine functions of everyday life.

Of course, these aides cannot give you an in-depth diagnosis of the resident's condition, nor should you expect it from them, but because they are in the closest and most frequent contact with the residents throughout the day, they can provide you with invaluable information about every aspect of daily life in the nursing home. If you treat them as allies and encourage them to share with you their unique knowledge of the residents, the reward will be more and better information for you and better care for your relative.

Common Problems to Watch For

Overmedication is the most pervasive resident-care problem in nursing homes today. The apathy, lethargy and mental deterioration that so many older people suffer in nursing homes can often be traced either wholly or in part to overmedication or to adverse drug reactions. These symptoms, of course, can have other causes as well, either organic or psychological. The emotional trauma of entering a nursing home, added to the psychological problem of coping with the illness or injury that made nursing home placement necessary, can often be more than enough to catapult the new resident into a severe depression. Still, any marked change in a nursing home resident's personality, attitude or mental capability should be reported immediately, and all possible causes, including overmedication or adverse drug reactions, should be thoroughly investigated. This is the area where the family's unique knowledge and active advocacy can be absolutely essential in ensuring that the last years of the resident's life will be as active and enjoyable as possible.

Difficulty in swallowing medications, either pills or thick liquids, is common among infirm elderly people. If a resident has this problem, the nurses should crush pills and mix them with apple sauce or jelly and dilute thick liquid medicines with juice or water. Because so many doctors do not specify these techniques in their prescriptions, it is up to the nurses to take the necessary steps to make certain that the residents can and do take their medications. Competent nurses should do this as a matter of course, but in some institutions residents are simply presented with the drugs in their original forms, which often remain unused. By arranging occasional visits to the home at a time when the resident is given medications, you can check to be sure they are administered effectively.

Bedsores or pressure sores (decubiti), a common hazard among bedridden or incontinent nursing home residents, are caused by the combination of pressure and moisture from urine and feces and tissue breakdown. These conditions, which occur when the patient is not turned regularly, massaged in specific areas or kept clean and dry at all times, produce ulceration and infection of the skin and soft tissue. Bedsores are painful and emit a foul-smelling discharge. They require immediate medical treatment to prevent possible enlargement.

An air mattress or waterbed can significantly reduce the danger of bedsores. You may want to purchase one for your relative as a preventive measure, but the best prevention against bedsores is prompt, attentive nursing care. If the older person is incontinent and confined to a wheelchair or a bed, find out how often aides routinely check incontinent residents and observe whether this task is being performed according to schedule. If you notice that she or he has urinated while you are visiting, immediately ask for assistance and monitor the time it takes for an aide to respond. Because failure to keep an incontinent and inactive resident clean and dry has such serious medical consequences, any problems of this kind should be reported to a supervisor.

If you have reason to suspect that your relative may be suffering from bedsores, conduct your own examination with the assistance of an aide if you want to be sure. Any signs of bedsores should be reported immediately to a nurse, who should chart them in the resident's medical record to ensure prompt treatment.

Foley catheters can cause serious urinary problems. When they are used for a prolonged period of time, special care is needed to avoid complications. If the resident is using a catheter, ask the nurse what precautions are being taken. If you suspect any problems, contact the resident's physician. Serious problems should be referred to a gynecologist or urologist.

Bruises or cuts may indicate that the resident was not handled properly by an aide or an orderly. Especially if your relative frequently has serious cuts and bruises, you should voice your concern and make every effort to determine what is causing them.

Before you jump to conclusions, however, you should bear in mind that as people grow older, their skin becomes thinner and less elastic. Their hands, arms and legs are unusually susceptible to cuts, bruises and skin tears. Even a small amount of pressure can cause a bruise that looks frighteningly large and serious, and a slight scratch can result in a nasty-looking cut. Many of the bruises and cuts suffered by nursing home residents are unavoidable, but some may be due to careless or even abusive treatment.

Unkempt fingernails and toenails are dangerous as well as unsightly for elderly people. Because their skin is so susceptible to cuts and bruises, nails should be kept clean and closely trimmed. Unfortunately, this is a chore that overtaxed nursing home aides may not get around to doing often enough for the resident's safety.

If you spot this problem, you should immediately express your concern to the aide responsible for your relative's personal care. If it recurs, you should report the problem to the head nurse. In some homes, you may even find it necessary to manicure the resident's nails yourself at regular intervals to ensure that it is done properly. You may also need to arrange to have a private podiatrist treat the older person periodically.

Bad breath, the most obvious sign of inadequate oral hygiene, is another problem frequently encountered in nursing homes. Since older people's gums easily become inflamed without thorough and regular brushing and flossing, or cleansing of dentures, you should check frequently to make sure the resident's teeth and gums are being cared for properly, and report any problems immediately. You may find it necessary to assume this responsibility yourself.

You should also check with the staff dentist or the resident's own dentist to ensure regular checkups. Make sure that the results are recorded in the medical records and that all prescribed treatments are performed.

CONSULTING WITH THE PROFESSIONAL STAFF

Conferences

Under the "Patient's Bill of Rights," which will be discussed more fully later in the chapter, residents and responsible family members have the right to be fully informed of the resident's medical condition and to participate in the planning of all treatment. Federal regulations mandate that nursing homes under government jurisdiction establish a detailed, written plan of care for each resident. Upon entering the home, the resident undergoes a thorough evaluation that includes both a complete medical examination and an exploration of all special needs, from dietary restrictions and preferences to social or emotional problems. Based on this professional evaluation, supplemented in the best homes by input from concerned family members, a planned regimen of total care is developed, including medications, medical treatments, diet, rehabilitative therapy and recommendations or precautions regarding participation in activities. The resident's personal physician, in consultation with the resident or a representative, should review the resident's plan of care at regular intervals and revise it as necessary. The Medicare program also requires, and many homes routinely schedule, periodic reassessments of the resident's need for nursing home care. Whenever there is any question about the continuing appropriateness of nursing home care, the family should discuss this issue thoroughly with the resident's physician and a social worker who is familiar with alternative services for the elderly in the community.

Many nursing homes actively invite the family's participation in planning and monitoring the resident's care by regularly scheduling conferences for family members, professional staff members and, if possible, the resident to review the plan for her or his care and to reassess the need for remaining in a nursing home. The first of these meetings is often a part of the admission process. If the home you have chosen does not schedule such conferences as a matter of course, you have the right to request that professional staff members review the plan of care with you at reasonable intervals.

These conferences provide the ideal opportunity to keep yourself well informed of the resident's medical condition and to raise any concerns you have regarding treatment and prog- ress. You can check on the kinds, quantities and possible side effects of medications the resident is being given. You can ask what program of rehabilitative therapy has been prescribed and how well the resident is responding. If either your own observa- tions or the information you receive from the professional staff indicates some problems, voicing your concern can lead to positive changes. During one routine conference, for example, Mr. Reed's family expressed their distress at seeing him acting more passive and lethargic and spending more time in bed. As a result of this discussion, the family, with the physician's approv- al, decided to invest in an air mattress to prevent bedsores, while the physician reduced the dosage of his medication and ordered an increased program of physical therapy. This joint effort soon resulted in a marked improvement in the resident's mental alertness and in his level of physical activity.

Because a nursing home is not only a medical facility but also the resident's home, the older person's emotional and mental state and social adjustment are equally important issues to explore on these occasions. Nursing home residents are often more likely to express their discomfort and dissatisfaction to close relatives and friends than to the staff. And the people closest to them are in the best position to see how well or poorly a resident is adjusting to life in the nursing home. If she or he is having problems, family members, with their intimate knowledge of their relative's personality, habits and feelings, may be better equipped than the most competent professional to identify the causes and to suggest possible remedies. By paying serious attention to the resident's emotional needs and communicating them to the staff clearly and effectively, the family can greatly enhance the quality of their relative's life in the home.

Physicians' Visits

In Medicare- and Medicaid-certified skilled nursing homes and in institutions licensed by most states as well, a physician must examine each resident at least once every thirty days and make a written evaluation of his or her progress. Whenever you have questions about the medical condition or treatment of your relative, you can ask when the doctor will visit the resident and arrange to be present at the time of the examination. If you can't always arrange to be there, you can communicate any questions in writing or by telephone.

Unfortunately, the quality of attention residents receive during their physician's visits varies widely. Regular attendance and active participation on your part is perhaps the single most effective step you can take to help ensure first-class medical attention.

Consultations with
Other Professional Staff Members

The head nurse or any of the registered nurses involved with the resident's care should also be able to keep you well informed about his or her medical condition and treatment plan. The nurses have far closer day-to-day contact than the physician, who may only see the resident once a month. For this reason, you are likely to find that nurses are quite sensitive to any changes in condition and needs. Because registered nurses are in charge of the day-to-day implementation of the resident's total plan of care, they should be willing to discuss a broad range of issues with you, from the resident's progress in rehabilitative therapy to emotional and social adjustments.

If you have serious concerns about these or other areas, you can always request individual consultations with the other professionals, including physical therapists, occupational therapists, social workers, activities directors, even podiatrists and dentists, who may work in the home, but whose paths may not ordinarily cross yours. As discussed in Chapter 3, the size, depth and quality of the professional staffs vary widely from one nursing home to another. The better informed you are of the professional resources of the particular home where your relative resides, the better equipped you will be to seek out and take advantage of the best possible care the home has to offer.

In all your dealings with the professional staff, you should bear in mind that, like professionals everywhere, they have many demands made on their time. If you corral a physician, nurse or physical therapist in the hall, you can't expect a serious half-hour or even five-minute consultation on the spot. Except in emergency situations, the best strategy is to request a brief appointment at their convenience.

Whenever you consult with professional staff members, either in person or on the telephone, try to make the conversation as clear and as brief as possible. Be sure to limit your questions and comments to the staff member's particular area of expertise and authority. Don't waste a physician's time by talking about the behavior of the resident's roommate or by complaining about an aide's failure to keep an incontinent resident dry when such concerns should be addressed to the head nurse. The more efficiently you can communicate your legitimate concerns to the right person, the more effective you will be as an advocate of the resident's best interests.

CHECKING THE MEDICAL RECORDS

In today's nursing homes, medical records are the primary means of communication among the various professionals who are responsible for any individual resident's care. Although by law all medical records must be treated as confidential, both the resident himself and the family member (or other responsible party who is chosen to serve as a representative) have the right to see them. If you learn how to use them, these records can become your single best source of current, reliable information about your relative's condition and the treatment received in the home.

A resident's permanent medical record begins when he or she is admitted to the nursing home. At that time, four important documents are entered into the records: the resident's medical history and findings of the physical examination; a psychological evaluation; the plan of care prescribed for the resident; and an activity plan (including medical permission forms, if necessary). Because these documents determine, at least initially, every facet of the resident's treatment plan, you should be familiar with what they contain. During your initial conference with the resident's physician or the head nurse, you should ask for a careful review of these documents to make certain you understand and accept the proposed plan.

MONITORING THE RESIDENT'S CARE

After the resident enters the home, the nursing home is required to maintain permanent records (either typed or legibly written in ink) that include, in addition to the documents already mentioned and various other forms, the following pieces of information, all of which can be eminently useful to monitor the resident's condition and care received:

1. Physician's notes on each visit, including diagnoses and orders for drugs, treatment (including rehabilitative therapy) and diet
2. Progress reports from professional consultants (e.g., podiatrist, occupational therapist), written at the time of each visit
3. Laboratory and X-ray reports
4. Log of resident's daily routine (including vital signs and body functions)
5. Weight log
6. Nurses' notes, which must include: care and treatment administered; resident's response to care and treatment; daily observation of how the resident looks, feels, reacts and interacts, as well as degree of dependency and motivation toward improved health; medications, their rationale, dosages, time and method of administration; type of restraint, if any, and time of its application and removal. (More and more states are also requiring weekly notes on the psychological, emotional, social, spiritual and recreational needs of the resident.)

Somewhere in the resident's medical records are answers to virtually all the questions you could possibly want to ask about her or his day-to-day condition, treatment, habits and responses. But since these records contain such a wealth of documentation, all of it written in more or less arcane jargon, your first glance at them can easily leave you feeling so overwhelmed and intimidated that you never ask to see them again. By giving up too quickly, however, you would deprive yourself of the single most valuable resource for independently monitoring your relative's care.

Although the medical records are written by professionals for other professionals and staff members in a language that is sometimes unfamiliar to the layperson, you can easily learn to use them for your own purposes. The first thing you need to learn is where to find the information you want. The most efficient way to accomplish this is in a brief conference with a registered nurse. If you begin by explaining that you want to review the resident's medical records frequently, so that you can keep abreast of his progress without demanding too much time from the professional staff, she should be glad to cooperate with you. A few questions such as these will quickly show you how the records are organized:

- Where will I find the physician's most recent recommendations?
- Where is the evidence that his or her orders were acted upon?
- Where can I find reports on the progress of the resident's rehabilitation therapy?
- Where is the resident's food and fluid intake recorded?

Once you've familiarized yourself with the system of medical record-keeping, the only remaining problem is figuring out how to decode the notations you do not immediately understand. The world of nursing homes, like most other businesses and professions, has both its set of acronyms and its own particular meanings for apparently familiar words. In a physical therapist's report, you may find the cryptic note "ROM: active-assistive," which translates into "range of motion: partial voluntary motion of a joint." Nurses' notes may include daily comments on your loved one's "R.O." These initials stand for "reality orientation," which, in nursing home jargon, refers to a program designed to help disoriented or brain-damaged patients compensate for diminished mental capabilities.

Appendix B of this book provides a glossary of terms and abbreviations commonly used in nursing homes. If you take it with you the first few times you go over your relative's medical records, it will help you understand many of the terms you encounter. A nurse should be willing to explain notations you can't decipher on your own. After a short while, you'll easily master this new vocabulary, and a quick check through the medical records will become a brief and painless part of your visits.

This is by far the most thorough and reliable way of monitoring a nursing home resident's physical condition and medical treatment. However helpful they may wish to be, staff nurses and the resident's personal physician simply cannot afford the time to review these medical records thoroughly and give concerned relatives a full report once a week, or even once a month. If your relative suddenly starts refusing physical therapy, for instance, it's quite possible that no one would think of mentioning it to you for weeks or even months. If you read his or her medical records weekly, however, you can take action to find out why the "resident does not respond" or "refuses to cooperate" and to push for a speedy solution to the problem. Checking the records yourself on a regular basis is the only way you can be sure that you will quickly learn of every significant change in the condition and treatment of your relative and be able to intervene, if necessary, as soon as possible.

Even if you prefer to use nurses, aides and the resident's personal physician as your chief sources of information about your relative's medical condition and treatment, it is still wise to check the medical records from time to time, to make sure they are both current and complete. Gaps in record-keeping can mean gaps in communication between the physician and staff members responsible for carrying out his or her orders. Especially if the resident is unaware that orders are being neglected or is unable to insist that they be carried out correctly, it is up to you, as the representative, to do so. Because thorough documentation is so essential to quality care in today's nursing homes, you should report any serious deficiencies in record-keeping to the head nurse or, if necessary, to the administrator.

OTHER WAYS TO MONITOR CARE

In addition to talking with the resident, consulting with staff members and checking the medical records, there are a number of other things you can do on your own to monitor care. Even if your schedule does not permit long and frequent visits to the nursing home, these precautions will help keep you in touch with the resident's condition, treatment and activities in the home.

Purchasing Medications

You can closely monitor the medications the resident is being given, and save some money as well, simply by arranging to purchase all prescribed drugs and take them, sealed, to the home. If you have a notation to this effect placed in the resident's medical record, this will ensure that you will always know exactly which medications and what dosages are being prescribed for the resident and that you will be immediately alerted to any changes in medication. By noting the dates when you fill or refill the prescriptions and the number of days the supply should last, you will also have an easy way of checking whether the medications are actually being administered to the resident on the proper schedule, which can be a problem in some nursing homes.

Doing the Resident's Laundry

Most nursing homes will be glad to arrange for you to do the resident's laundry at home. This will save you money and help prevent belongings from being lost, misplaced or stolen. It will also be far easier on the clothes, because state laws require that nursing home laundries use sterilizing temperatures. And, above all, it will give you an additional way of monitoring the personal care the resident is receiving.

Anyone who has ever tried to dress a severely crippled older person knows what a time-consuming struggle it can be. Even in the best nursing homes, overworked aides may not expend the energy it takes to coax and wrestle a resident out of bed and into his or her clothes every day. On the days the older person is not expecting visitors and has no particular reason to get up, she or he can quickly succumb to the routine of spending most days in bed. Within weeks, this inactivity can cause severe damage both to morale and to physical strength.

The simple expedient of doing the resident's laundry affords you a virtually foolproof way of monitoring this all-important area of personal care on days when you are not present at the home. If several changes of street clothes need laundering in a week, for instance, you will be assured that your relative is frequently up and about. If very few street clothes need washing, you will have good reason to believe that he or she is probably spending too much time in bed and is not being dressed every day. By recognizing this early warning sign of neglect as soon as it appears, you can take steps to prevent the irreversible emotional and physical deterioration that too often needlessly afflicts nursing home residents.

Reviewing the Bills

Paying the bills in person is an excellent way of keeping in contact with the administrative staff. The more staff members who are concerned about every aspect of your relative's life in the nursing home, the better the care is likely to be.

Before you pay each nursing home bill, you should carefully review each item. Ancillary charges, which can include a wheelchair, commode or other equipment rental and a wide range of medical and personal care supplies, merit particularly close attention. You should feel free to question any items that strike you as unusual or inappropriate in order to make sure that your loved one is actually receiving those extra services or supplies. By checking each bill carefully and investigating any new or surprising items, you will protect yourself against mistaken or deliberate overcharges. And you may also learn about changes in the resident's condition and needs that would not otherwise have come to your attention.

KNOWING THE RESIDENT'S RIGHTS—AND YOUR OWN

To represent your relative's interests effectively, you should be thoroughly familiar with the rights of nursing home residents and their representatives under federal law. Largely in response to the deplorable conditions found in some nursing homes, in 1974 the Department of Health, Education and Welfare issued regulations establishing the legal rights of nursing home residents and the standard of care to which they are entitled. Homes that are not federally licensed under the Medicare or Medicaid programs are not required to adhere to these regulations, but most good homes do so voluntarily. The laws of many states also provide similar protection for nursing home residents.

Commonly referred to as the "Patient's Bill of Rights," these federal regulations designed to protect the rights of residents in skilled nursing facilities can be summarized as follows.* Residents have the right:

1. to be fully informed of their rights and of all the rules and regulations of the nursing home regarding resident conduct;

Code of Federal Regulations

2. to be fully informed of the services available in the home and of the charges for such services;

3. to be fully informed by a physician of their medical condition; to have the opportunity to participate in the planning of their medical treatment and to refuse to participate in experimental research;

4. to refuse treatment to the extent permitted by law and to be informed of the medical consequences of such a refusal;

5. to be transferred or discharged only for medical reasons, or for their own welfare or that of other residents, or for nonpayment of fees, or because they so desire, and to be given reasonable advance notice to ensure orderly transfer or discharge (such actions must be documented in their health records);

6. to be encouraged and assisted to exercise their rights as residents and as citizens; to this end to be able to voice grievances and recommend changes in policies to home staff or outside representatives, free from restraint or interference;

7. to manage their personal financial affairs, or, if the facility is assigned this responsibility, to be given an accounting (at least quarterly) of any financial transactions made on their behalf;

8. to be free from mental and physical abuse and from chemical and physical restraints except as authorized in writing by a physician for a specified period of time or, in emergency situations, when necessary to protect the resident from personal injury or injury to others;

9. to be assured of confidential treatment of their personal and medical records, and to approve or refuse release of the records to anyone outside the home, except in the case of transfer to another health facility or as required by law or third-party contract;

10. to be treated with consideration, respect and full recogni-

tion of their dignity and individuality, including privacy in treatment and care for their personal needs;

11. not to be required to perform services for the home (such as washing floors or windows) that are not included in the plan of care for therapeutic purposes;
12. to associate and communicate privately with persons of their own choice, and to send out and receive personal mail unopened;
13. to retain and use personal clothing and possessions as space permits, unless this would infringe upon the rights of other residents;
14. if married, to be assured privacy for visits from spouses, and, if both are residents in the home, to be permitted to share a room;
15. to have daily visiting hours established;
16. to have members of the clergy admitted at the request of the resident or family representative at any time;
17. to have relatives or close friends visit critically ill residents at any time;
18. to be allowed privacy for visits with family, friends, clergy and social workers, for professional or business purposes;
19. to have reasonable access to telephones both to make and to receive confidential calls;
20. to be permitted to purchase drugs and rent or purchase medical supplies or equipment in accordance with the provisions of Section 1320 of the Health and Safety Code.

New information should become available as various groups study nursing homes and their compliance with regulations. (See Bibliography, Karby Davidson's "Nursing Home Residents Given Voice.")

An individual resident's rights may be denied or limited only for good cause and by order of his or her physician. Any such denial or limitation must be documented by the attending physician in the resident's medical record.

For family members concerned with monitoring the resident's care in the nursing home, *it is extremely important to know that the first four of these rights are also delegated to the resident's guardian, next of kin, or sponsoring agency,* particularly (but not exclusively) in cases when the resident is aphasic, disoriented or otherwise incapable of understanding her or his rights. Some older people who enter a nursing home are capable of making their own decisions and representing their own interests, but many are not. In these cases, the resident's rights and responsibilities are transferred to his or her designated representative, who is authorized to act on the older person's behalf. The representative may be a spouse, a family member or friend, a legal guardian or conservator, a sponsoring agent or agencies, or even the trust department of a bank.

Obviously, the nursing home resident's interests are best served if the authorized representative is a caring family member or friend who lives nearby and has the time and energy to become actively involved. If you are willing to take on this responsibility, the Patient's Bill of Rights ensures that you will have the authority to represent your loved one's interests effectively. As the designated representative, you will have the right to be fully informed of a patient's medical condition, to participate in shaping a plan of care and to refuse treatment to the extent permitted by law. In effect, the resident's personal physician and the nursing home staff are legally responsible to you and obliged to cooperate with your efforts to see that your loved one is receiving quality care.

DEALING WITH COMPLAINTS

Even in the best homes, situations can arise that require a resident's representative to take strong corrective action. Confronted with evidence of possible abuse or neglect, concerned relatives or friends are often tempted to remain silent, fearing that expressing their displeasure may alienate the staff and ultimately harm the resident more than it will help. These fears generally stem from the well-publicized horror stories of nursing home abuses that began appearing in the sixties. Complaints of mistreatment sometimes subjected the resident to reprisals in the form of verbal or physical abuse or neglect. It was not uncommon for administrators to shrug off complaints with the attitude "If you're not satisfied, you'd better go elsewhere." Although these attitudes and practices have not been totally eradicated, they have become increasingly rare as nursing homes, under the pressure of government legislation and continuing consumer advocacy, have become more accountable to federal and state authorities and more responsive to their clients. Today, a resident stands a far better chance of receiving quality care if her or his representative is willing to speak up whenever necessary than if everyone simply keeps quiet and hopes for the best.

Resolving Complaints Within the Home

Many of today's nursing homes are actively encouraging frank, open discussion of problems. Some have grievance committees or councils on which the resident and his or her representative meet with staff members, and sometimes other residents as well, for the purpose of resolving problems within the home. Others have an official ombudsman who is responsible for mediating disputes involving residents' complaints. Whether or not your relative's home has established such formal grievance procedures, you are likely to find staff members willing to cooperate with your efforts to correct any deficiencies in the resident's care if you approach them with the proper attitude.

By making judicious use of questions, suggestions and simple statements, you can resolve many problems without stirring up the negative feelings incited by accusations or demands. As long as you continue being civil and respectful to everyone who takes the time to discuss your concerns with you, you will stand an excellent chance of resolving the immediate problem without jeopardizing either the resident's or your own positive relationships with the nursing home staff.

Once you are convinced that you have a legitimate complaint that requires corrective action, make the effort to work through proper channels, rather than immediately reporting your suspicions of misconduct to the director of nursing or the home's administrator. Many problems can be resolved effectively and diplomatically by discussing your concern with the aide directly responsible for the resident's care. If you have reason to believe that your relative was bruised by rough handling, for instance, simply ask the aides involved with recent care how the injury occurred; you're likely to receive a reasonable explanation that will allay your fears. As a result of your inquiry, the aides will be particularly cautious in the future, whether or not they were actually at fault on this occasion.

If your discussion with the aide does not allay your concern, you should report the problem to the staff nurse who supervises the aides and orderlies on that shift. Any serious complaint that cannot be resolved at this level should be referred, in turn, to the head nurse and then to the director of nursing, or to the head of the appropriate department if it is not a medical issue. The nursing home administrator is the authority of last resort within the home and is ultimately responsible for every aspect of resident care. Consequently, you should not hesitate to take your problem to her or him if you are unable to resolve it at a lower level.

The Nursing Home Ombudsman Program

If all your efforts to resolve a serious problem within the nursing home end in failure, you need not resign yourself to choosing between the undesirable alternatives of accepting inferior care or transferring your relative to another home. These days, dissatisfied nursing home residents and their families have a powerful ally in the Nursing Home Ombudsman Program. Established as part of the federal government's Comprehensive Older American Act of 1978, the Nursing Home Ombudsman Program is administered by state offices on aging. One of its primary functions is to investigate and resolve complaints made by or on behalf of older people who are residents of skilled nursing homes and intermediate care facilities.

The case of Mr. White illustrates how helpful the intervention of a nursing home ombudsman can be. Eighty-five and senile, Mr. White was subjected to a constant stream of abuse from his roommate, to his family's dismay. After trying to reason with the roommate, to no avail, the family complained to the head nurse, whose unsympathetic response was, "So what? Your father is senile. He doesn't know the difference." With a complaint about the head nurse's attitude added to their initial concern about the roommate, the family then approached the home's administrator, who fully supported the head nurse and dismissed the problem as trivial. At this point, the family wrote a letter of complaint to the state ombudsman program. Within a week, the ombudsman was on hand to resolve the difficulties. The roommate was moved to a single room, the administrator was given a warning, and the head nurse, who had several complaints on her record, was dismissed.

To find the ombudsman program office that serves your area, look in the yellow pages of the phone book under "Nursing Homes" or "Senior Centers"; or in the white pages or government pages under "Department of Aging," "Government Offices" or "Department of Social Services." If you don't find an office in your immediate vicinity, contact the state headquarters of the Nursing Home Ombudsman Program for the office nearest you. Appendix A lists the addresses and telephone numbers of each state's program office.

Other Ways of Registering Complaints Against Nursing Homes

Nursing homes today are accountable to many state, local and professional organizations. If you have a serious complaint against a nursing home, you can effectively voice your dissatisfaction by contacting at least some, if not all, of the following:

1. Your local Social Security office, which functions as clearinghouse for complaints about all nursing homes, whether or not they receive government funds
2. Your county welfare office (if the resident is covered by Medicaid)
3. The state Medicaid agency (if the home is certified for that program)
4. The state health department and the state nursing home licensing authority
5. The state board that licenses nursing home administrators
6. Your local hospital association and medical society
7. The American Health Care Association or the Joint Commission on Accreditation of Hospitals, if the home is accredited by either of these organizations
8. Your local Better Business Bureau, Chamber of Commerce or Consumer Complaint Agency
9. Your local and state elected representatives
10. The local district attorney's office

Well-documented letters of complaint to one or more of these authorities can have a considerable impact, especially if you send copies to the administrator of the nursing home. Even those few administrators, who are more concerned with the bottom line than with the welfare of the residents, care greatly about the home's reputation and their own, to say nothing of eligibility for licensing and accreditation. Showing that you are willing and able to make your complaints public gives an administrator a powerful incentive to satisfy your legitimate demands.

If letters of complaint do not succeed in correcting the immediate problem, they still serve an important function. Nursing homes are far better than they were twenty years ago because of increased governmental vigilance, media attention and consumer pressure. By bringing serious complaints against nursing homes to the attention of the proper authorities, you can contribute to this continuing social effort to make nursing home abuses a thing of the past, and to ensure quality care for all our elderly citizens.

Afterword

Death lies beyond the scope of this book. Furthermore, the subjects of death and bereavement have been covered in depth by a number of fine writers in that field.

One of the foremost is Elizabeth Kubler-Ross. In her influential work, *Death and Dying,* she offers a framework for understanding the emotional responses of people who are facing death and the parallel reactions of their loved ones.

In further response to the needs of the bereaved, numerous support groups and counseling programs are conducted by hospitals, community health agencies, senior citizen centers and civic organizations.

Finally, the advice and experience related in this book reflect hindsight. I only wish that what is in these pages could have been available to me during the ordeal that preceded my mother's death.

It gives me genuine pleasure to know that, with this book in hand, the reader can face bewildering circumstances squarely and work knowledgeably through each of them, step by step.

Bibliography

Alexander, G. J., "Who Benefits from Conservatorship?" *Trial* 13 (May 1977), pp. 30–32.

Brown, Robert N. *The Rights of Older Persons*. New York: Avon Books, 1979.

————. "An Appraisal of the Nursing Home Enforcement Process." *Arizona Law Review* 17 (1975), p. 304.

Barrow, Georgia M., and Patricia A. Smith. *Aging, Ageism, and Society*. New York: West Publishing Co., 1979.

Bennett, Clifford. *Nursing Home Life: What It Is, and What It Could Be*. New York: Tiresias Press, 1980.

Beyer, Jane, Josephine Bulkley and Paula Hopkins. *A Model Act Regulating Board and Care Homes: Guidelines for States*. Washington, D.C.: The American Bar Association's Commission on Legal Problems of the Elderly and the Commission on the Mentally Disabled, 1984.

Birren, James E., and K. Warner Schoie, eds. *The Handbook of the Psychology of Aging*. New York: Van Nostrand Reinhold Company, 1977.

Brickner, Philip W., M.D. *Home Health Care for the Aged: How to Help Older People Stay in Their Own Homes and Out of Institutions*. New York: Appleton-Century-Crofts, 1978.

Brody, Elaine. *Long-Term Care of Older People: A Practical Guide*. New York: Human Sciences Press, 1977.

Brody, Jane E. *Jane Brody's New York Times Guide to Personal Health*. New York: Avon Books, 1983.

————. "Nursing Homes: A Guide to Picking One That Best Meets a Patient's Needs." *San Francisco Chronicle,* January 6, 1982, reprinted from *The New York Times.*

————. "Personal Health: Good Care at Home." *The New York Times,* Wednesday, September 3, 1980.

Brown, R. N. "Aging in America. A Bill of Rights for Nursing Home Patients." *Trial* 13 (May 1977), pp. 22–28.

Brunner, Lilian Sholtis and Doris Smith Suddarth. *Textbook of Medical-Surgical Nursing,* Fourth Edition. Philadelphia: J. B. Lippincott, 1980.

Buckingham, Robert W. *The Complete Hospice Guide.* New York: Harper & Row, 1983.

Burger, Sarah, Sarah Greene and Martha D'Erasmo. *Living in a Nursing Home.* New York: Seabury Press, 1976.

Burnside, Irene. *Working with the Elderly: Group Process and Technique.* Belmont, CA: Wadsworth Press, 1978.

Butler, R. N. *Why Survive? Being Old in America.* New York: Harper & Row, 1975.

Code of Federal Regulations. 42: Public Health, Part 400 to End, U.S. Government Printing Office, Washington, D.C., The Office of the Federal Register, National Archives and Record Services, General Services Administration, 1980.

Comfort, Alex. *A Good Age.* New York: Simon and Schuster, 1976.

Cousins, Norman. *Anatomy of an Illness.* New York: Bantam Books, 1979.

Crandall, Richard C. *Gerontology.* Menlo Park, CA: Addison-Wesley, 1979.

Curtin, Sharon R. *Nobody Ever Died of Old Age: In Praise of Old People.* Boston: Atlantic Monthly Press, 1972.

Deedy, John. *Your Aging Parent.* Chicago: Thomas More Press, 1984.

Fischer, David Hacket. *Growing Old in America.* London: Oxford University Press, 1978.

Fisk, Albert A. *A New Look at Senility.* Springfield, IL: Charles C. Thomas, 1981.

Fitzharris, T. L. *The Desirability of a Correctional Ombudsman.* Berkeley: Institute of Government Studies, University of California, 1973.

Freeman, I. T. *Aging: Its History and Literature.* New York: Human Sciences Press, 1979.

Gelfand, Donald, and James Olsen. *The Aging Network: Programs and Services for the Elderly.* New York: Spring Publishing Co., 1980.

Gelman, David, et al. "Who's Taking Care of Our Parents?" *Newsweek.* May 6, 1985, pp. 60–70.

General Accounting Office, Comptroller General, Report to Congress. *Entering a Nursing Home—Costly Implications for Medicaid and the Elderly.* General Accounting Office, PAD-80-12, Washington, D.C., November 26, 1979.

Hodkinson, H. M. *An Outline of Geriatrics*. New York: Grune and Stratton, 1981.

————. *Common Symptoms of Disease in the Elderly*, 2nd ed. New York: Blackwell Scientific Publications, 1980.

Hoeker, E. T. "Expansion of Health Care Providers' Liability: An Application of *Darling* to Long-Term Health Care Facilities." *Connecticut Law Review* 9 (Spring 1977), pp. 462–81.

Horner, Joyce. *That Time of Year: A Chronicle of Life in a Nursing Home*. Cambridge, MA: University of Massachusetts Press, 1982.

ICSG, International Center for Social Gerontology, Inc. *Assisted Independent Living in Residential Congregate Housing for Older People: A Report on the Situation in the United States*, Parts III and IV. Washington, D.C.: ICSG, 1978.

Karby Davidson, Sandra. "Nursing Home Residents Given Voice." *AARP News Bulletin*, Vol. XXVII, No. 6, June 1986.

Koff, Theodore. *Hospice: A Caring Community*. Cambridge, MA: Winthrop Publishers, 1980.

Kubler-Ross, Elizabeth. *Living with Death and Dying*. New York: Macmillan, 1981.

————. *On Death and Dying*. New York: Macmillan, 1969.

———— and Mal Warshaw. *Working It Through*. New York: Macmillan, 1982.

Lesnoff-Caravaglia, Gari. *Health Care of the Elderly*. New York: Human Sciences Press, 1980.

Libow, L. S., and F. T. Sherman, eds. *The Core of Geriatric Medicine: A Guide for Students and Practitioners*. St. Louis, MO: C.V. Mosby, 1981.

Mace, Nancy L., and Peter V. Robins, M.D. *The 36-Hour Day*. New York: Warner Books, 1984.

Mendelson, Mary Adelaide. *Tender Loving Greed*. New York: Alfred A. Knopf, 1974.

Miller, Dulcy, and Susan Beer. "Patterns of Friendship Among Patients in a Nursing Home Setting." *Gerontologist*, Vol. 17, 1977, pp. 269–275.

Moss, F. E., and V. Halamandaris. *Too Old, Too Sick, Too Bad: Nursing Homes in America*. Germantown, MO: Aspen Systems Corp., 1977.

National Institute of Adult Daycare. *A Directory of Daycare Programs in the United States*. Washington, D.C.: National Institute of Adult Daycare, 1980.

Nascher, L. L. *Geriatrics, the Diseases of Old Age and Their Treatment*. Philadelphia: P. Blakiston and Sons, 1914.

Nassau, Jean Baron. *Choosing a Nursing Home*. New York: Funk & Wagnalls, 1975.

Notelovitz, Morris, M.D., Ph.D., and Marsha Ware. *Stand Tall!* Gainsville, FL: Triad Publishing Company, 1982.

BIBLIOGRAPHY

"Nursing Home Liability." *American Jurisprudence Proof of Facts* 27, p. 623.

O'Hara-Deveraux, Mary, et al., eds. *Eldercare: A Guide to Clinical Geriatrics*. New York: Grune and Stratton, 1981.

Otten, Jane, and Florence D. Shelley. *When Your Parents Grow Old*. New York: Signet, 1978.

Regan, J. J. "When Nursing Home Patients Complain: The Ombudsman or the Patient Advocate?" *Georgetown Law Journal* 65 (Fall 1977), pp. 691–738.

Reichel, William, M.D., ed. *Topics in Aging and Long-Term Care*. Baltimore, MD: Williams and Wilkins Co., 1981.

—————. *The Geriatric Patient*. New York: Hospital Practice Publishing Co., 1978.

Robertson, John A. *The Rights of the Critically Ill*. New York: Bantam Books, 1983.

Rossman, Isadore, ed. *Clinical Geriatrics*. New York: Lippincott, 1979.

Rubenstein, Laurence Z., et al. "Effectiveness of a Geriatric Unit: A Randomized Clinical Trial." *The New England Journal of Medicine*, Vol. 311, pp. 1664–1670.

Scott, Russell. *The Body As Property*. New York: Viking Press, 1981.

Second Conference on the Epidemiology of Aging. (NIH Publication No. 80-969), Washington, D.C.: U.S. Government Printing Office, 1980.

Sherwood, Sylvia, et al. *An Alternative to Institutionalization: The Highland Heights Experiment*. Cambridge, MA: Ballinger Publishing Co., 1981.

Silverstone, Barbara, and Helen Kandel Hyman. *You and Your Aging Parent*. New York: Pantheon Books, 1982.

Smith, Bert Kruger. *The Pursuit of Dignity*. Boston: Beacon Press, 1977.

Stacy, F. *Ombudsman Compared*. Oxford: Clarendon Press, 1978.

Taeuber, Cynthia M. *An Aging Society*. Washington, D.C.: U.S. Department of Commerce, 1983.

Trocchis, J. *Home Care for the Elderly: A Guide for Those Who Are Considering Care for Elderly Relatives at Home*. Boston: CBI Publishing Co., 1980.

U.S. Congress. Senate. Special Committee on Aging, Subcommittee on Long-Term Care. *Nursing Home Care in the United States: Failure in Public Policy*. Supporting Paper No. 7, "The Role of Nursing Homes in Caring for Discharged Mental Patients (and the Birth of a For-Profit Boarding Home Industry)." 94th Congress, 2nd Session, March 1976. Washington, D.C.: Government Printing Office, 1976.

U.S. Congress. Senate. Special Committee on Aging, Subcommittee on Long-Term Care. *Nursing Home Care in the United States: Failure in Public Policy*. Supporting Paper No. 5, "The Continuing Chronicle of Nursing

Home Fires." 94th Congress, 1st Session, August 1975. Washington, D.C.: Government Printing Office, 1975. (Report No. 94-000)

U.S. Congress. Senate. Special Committee on Aging. Subcommittee on Long-Term Care. *Nursing Home Care in the United States: Failure in Public Policy.* Supporting Paper No. 6, "What Can be Done in Nursing Homes: Positive Aspects in Long-Term Care." 94th Congress, 1st Session, September 1975. Washington, D.C.: Government Printing Office, 1975.

U.S. Department of Health and Human Services, Office of Human Development Services, Administration on Aging. *Aging 1981,* Nos. 321-322. Washington, D.C.: 1981 (DHHS) Pub. No. (OHD) (AOA) 81-20949.

U.S. Department of Health and Human Services, Public Health Service, National Institutes of Health. *Q & A: Alzheimer's Disease.* (Reprinted by Alzheimer's Disease and Related Disorders Association, Inc., 360 North Michigan Avenue, Suite 601, Chicago, IL 60601. NIH Publication No. 80-1646, June 1981.)

U.S. Department of Health and Human Services, Social Security Administration, Health Care Financing Administration. *A Brief Explanation of Medicare.* SSA Publication No. 05-10043. Washington, D.C.: May 1980.

U.S. Department of Health, Education, and Welfare, Health Care Financing Administration, Health Standards and Quality Bureau. *Activities Coordinator's Guide: A Handbook for Activities Coordinators in Long-Term Care Facilities.* HCFA-HSQB 78-004.

U.S. Department of Health, Education, and Welfare, Health Care Financing Administration, Health Standards and Quality Bureau, Office of Standards and Certification. *Manual of Survey Techniques and Practices, A Guide to Surveying Medicare-Medicaid Standards for Skilled Nursing Facilities.* DHEW Contract HSM 110-70-311. Washington, D.C.: April 1978.

U.S. Department of Health, Education, and Welfare, Health Care Financing Administration, Medical Services Administration. *Nursing Home Care.* HCFA 77-24902. Washington, D.C.: Revised 1976-77.

U.S. Department of Health, Education, and Welfare, Office of Human Development Services, Administration on Aging, National Clearing House on Aging. *Facts About Older Americans 1978,* DHEW Pub. No. (OHDC) 79-20006 (GPO). Washington, D.C.: September 1976.

U.S. Department of Health, Education, and Welfare, Social Security Administration, Health Care Financing Administration. *Your Medicare Handbook.* SSA Publication No. 05-10050. Washington, D.C.: January 1980.

U.S. Department of Health, Education, and Welfare, Social Security Administration, Health Care Financing Administration. *Medicare Coverage in a Skilled Nursing Facility.* SSA Publication No. 05-10041, GPO 1980: 620-329/53. Washington, D.C.: February 1980.

U.S. Department of Health, Education, and Welfare, Social Security Adminis-

BIBLIOGRAPHY

tration, Health Care Financing Administration. *Home Health Care Under Medicare*. HEW Publication No. (SSA) 80-10042, GPO 1980 670-329/78. Washington, D.C.: September 1979.

U.S. Department of Health, Education, and Welfare, Health Care Financing Administration. *Guide to Health Insurance for People with Medicare*. Developed Jointly by the National Association of Insurance Commissioners and the Health Care Financing Administration of the U.S. Department of Health, Education, and Welfare. HCFA-02110. Washington, D.C.: December 1979.

U.S. Senate, Special Committee on Aging. *Health Care for Older Americans: The "Alternatives" Issues*. Washington, D.C.: U.S. Government Printing Office, 1977.

Wishard, Laurie and William. *60 Plus in California*. San Francisco: Cragmont Publications, 1981.

Appendix A

WHERE TO FIND HELP

I. *FAMILY SERVICE AGENCIES*

The Family Service Association of America can direct you to the Family Service Agencies in your area. They also publish an annual *Directory of Member Agencies*.

Family Service Association of America
44 East 23rd Street
New York, NY 10010
(212) 674-6100

II. *NURSING HOME ORGANIZATIONS*

The American Association of Homes for the Aging (AAHA) represents only nonprofit nursing homes. The American Health Care Association represents proprietary, for-profit nursing homes as well as nonprofit nursing homes. Both furnish lists of homes affiliated with their organizations and accredited by them.

American Association of Homes for the Aging (AAHA)
1050 17th Street, N.W., Suite 770
Washington, D.C. 20036
(202) 296-5960

American Health Care Association (AHCA)
1200 15th Street, N.W.
Washington, D.C. 20005
(202) 833-2050

III. *DIRECTORY OF LONG-TERM CARE OMBUDSMAN OFFICES*

CENTRAL OFFICE

Office of State and Tribal Programs
Administration on Aging
Office of Human Development Services
U.S. Department of Health and Human Services
330 Independence Avenue, S.W.
Washington, D.C. 20201
(202) 245-1826

ALABAMA

Commission on Aging
Executive Park
2853 Fairlane Drive
Building G, Suite 63
Montgomery, AL 36130
(205) 832-6640

ALASKA

Alaska Project Director's Association
1577 C Street
Anchorage, AK 99501
(907) 279-2232

ARIZONA

Aging and Adult Administration
1400 W. Washington St.
P.O. Box 6123
Phoenix, AZ 85007
(602) 255-4446

ARKANSAS

Office on Aging and Adult Services
Department of Human Services
Donaghey Building
7th and Main
Little Rock, AR 72201
(501) 271-8167
1-800-482-8049 (in state)

CALIFORNIA
Department on Aging
1020 19th Street
Sacramento, CA 95814
(916) 323-6681

COLORADO
**Medical Care and Research
Foundation**
1565 Clarkson Street
Denver, CO 80218
(303) 830-7744

CONNECTICUT
Department of Aging
80 Washington Street
Hartford, CT 06106
(203) 566-7770

DELAWARE
Supportive Community Services, Inc.
903 Washington Street
Wilmington, DE 19801
(302) 655-3451

DISTRICT OF COLUMBIA
Office on Aging
1424 K Street, N.W., Second Floor
Washington, D.C. 20005
(202) 724-5622

FLORIDA
State Long-Term Care Ombudsman Committee
Department of Health & Rehabilitation Services
1317 Winewood Boulevard
Building 1, Box 309
Tallahassee, FL 32301
(904) 488-4180

GEORGIA
Office of Aging
Department of Human Resources
618 Ponce de Leon Avenue, N.E.
Atlanta, GA 30308
(404) 894-5336

HAWAII
Office of the Governor
1149 Bethel Street, Room 307
Honolulu, HI 96813
(808) 548-2593

IDAHO
Office on Aging
Statehouse, Room 114
Boise, ID 83720
(208) 334-3833

ILLINOIS
Department on Aging
421 E. Capitol Avenue
Springfield, IL 62706
(217) 785-1568

INDIANA
**Indiana Department on
  Aging and Community
  Services**
115 N. Penn Street, Suite 1350
Indianapolis, IN 46204
(317) 232-1203

IOWA
Commission on Aging
415 W. 10th Street
Des Moines, IA 50319
(515) 281-5187

KANSAS
Department on Aging
610 W. 10th Street
Topeka, KS 66612
(913) 296-4986

KENTUCKY
**Department for Aging
  Services**
275 E. Main Street
Frankfort, KY 40601
(502) 564-5498

LOUISIANA
Office of Elderly Affairs
P.O. Box 80374
Baton Rouge, LA 70989
(504) 342-2764

MAINE
Committee on Aging
State House
Augusta, ME 04333
(207) 289-3658

MARYLAND
Office on Aging
301 W. Preston Street, Room
  1004
Baltimore, MD 21201
(301) 383-5064

MASSACHUSETTS
Department of Elder Affairs
38 Chauncey Street
Boston, MA 02111
(617) 727-7750

MICHIGAN
Office of Service to the Aging
300 E. Michigan
P.O. Box 30026
Lansing, MI 48933
(517) 482-1297

MINNESOTA
Board on Aging
Suite 204, Metro Square
  Building
75th & Robert Streets
St. Paul, MN 55101
(612) 296-2770

MISSISSIPPI
Council on Aging
301 Executive Building
802 N. State Street
Jackson, MS 39201
(601) 354-6590

MISSOURI
Office of Aging
P.O. Box 1337
Jefferson City, MO 65102
(314) 751-3082

MONTANA
**Seniors' Office of Legal &
Ombudsman Services**
P.O. Box 232, Capitol Station
Helena, MT 59620
(406) 449-5650

NEBRASKA
Department on Aging
P.O. Box 95044
Lincoln, NE 68509
(402) 471-2307

NEVADA
**Division of Aging Services
Department of Human
Resources**
505 E. King Street
Kinkead Building, Room 600
Carson City, NV 89710
(702) 885-4210

NEW HAMPSHIRE
**New Hampshire Council on
Aging**
P.O. Box 786
14 Depot Street
Concord, NH 03301
(603) 271-2751

NEW MEXICO
State Agency on Aging
440 St. Michaels Drive
Santa Fe, NM 87501
(505) 827-2802

NEW YORK
Office for the Aging
Agency Building #2
Empire State Plaza
Albany, NY 12223
(518) 474-5731

NORTH CAROLINA
**Division on Aging
Department of Human
Resources**
Administration Building
708 Hillsborough Street, Suite
200
Raleigh, NC 27603
(919) 733-2983

NORTH DAKOTA
Aging Services
Social Services Board
Bismarck, ND 58505
(701) 224-2577

OHIO
Commission on Aging
50 W. Broad Street, 9th Floor
Columbus, OH 43216
(614) 466-1220
1-800-282-1206

OKLAHOMA
Special Unit on Aging
Department of Human
  Services
P.O. Box 25352
Oklahoma City, OK 73125
(405) 521-2281

OREGON
Office of the Governor
160 C State Capitol
Salem, OR 97310
(503) 378-6533

PENNSYLVANIA
Department of Aging
231 State Street
Harrisburg, PA 17101
(717) 787-1352

PUERTO RICO
Gericulture Commission
Department of Social Services
P.O. Box 11398
Santurce, Puerto Rico 00910
(809) 722-2429
  (overseas operator)

RHODE ISLAND
Department of Elderly Affairs
79 Washington Street
Providence, RI 02903
(401) 277-6880

SAMOA
Territorial Administration on
  Aging
Government of American
  Samoa
Pago Pago, Tutuila
American Samoa 96799
Dial 9-0: ask for Oakland over-
  seas operator, Samoa 3-2121

SOUTH CAROLINA
Office of the Ombudsman
Governor's Office
1205 Pendleton Street
Edgar A. Brown Building
Columbia, SC 29201
(803) 758-8016

SOUTH DAKOTA
Office of Adult Services and
  Aging
Division of Human
  Development
Department of Social Services
700 North Illinois Street
Pierre, SD 57501-2291
(605) 773-3656

TENNESSEE
Commission on Aging
703 Tennessee Building
535 Church Street
Nashville, TN 37219
(615) 741-2056

TEXAS
Department on Aging
P.O. Box 12786, Capitol
  Stations
Austin, TX 78704
(512) 475-2717

UTAH
Division on Aging
Department of Social Services
150 West North Temple, Third
  Floor
Salt Lake City, UT 84102
(801) 533-6422

VIRGIN ISLANDS
**Government of the Virgin
  Islands**
Commission on Aging
P.O. Box 539
Charlotte Amalie
St. Thomas, Virgin Islands
  00801
(809) 774-5884 (overseas
  operator)

VERMONT
Office on Aging
103 South Main
Waterbury, VT 05676
(802) 241-2400

VIRGINIA
Office on Aging
830 East Main Street, Suite
  950
Richmond, VA 23219
(804) 786-7894

WASHINGTON
Division of Audit
Department of Social and Health
  Services
MS OB3-33B
Olympia, WA 98504
(206) 753-2501

WEST VIRGINIA
Commission on Aging
State Capitol
Charleston, WV 25305
(304) 348-3317

WISCONSIN
**Board on Aging and Long-
  Term Care**
819 North 6th, Room 270
Milwaukee, WI 53203
(414) 224-4386

APPENDIX A

WYOMING
Wyoming State Bar Association
Attention: OAAP
Hathaway Building
814 8th Street
Cheyenne, WY 82001
(307) 777-7561

IV. *ADVOCACY GROUPS FOR THE ELDERLY*

American Association of Retired Persons (AARP)
1909 K Street, N.W.
Washington, D.C. 20049
Founded 1958

Gray Panthers National Office
3635 Chestnut Street
Philadelphia, PA 19104
Founded 1971

Legal Counsel for the Elderly (LCE)
Sponsored by AARP
1909 K Street, N.W.
Washington, D.C. 20036
Founded 1975

National Caucus & Center on Black Aged
1424 K Street, N.W., Suite 500
Washington, D.C. 20005
Founded 1980

National Citizens' Coalition for Nursing Home Reform (NCCNHR)
1825 Connecticut Avenue, N.W., Suite 417B
Washington, D.C. 20009
Founded 1975

National Council of Senior Citizens (NCSC)
1309 L Street, N.W.
Washington, D.C. 20005
Founded 1961

National Senior Citizen Law Center (NSCLC)
1302 18th Street, N.W., Suite 701
Washington, D.C. 20036
Founded 1972

Older Women's League (OWL)
1325 G St. N.W., LLB
Washington, D.C. 20005
Founded 1980

V. *FOUNDATIONS CONCERNED WITH AGING (OR THE ELDERLY)*

Abbott Laboratories Fund
Abbott Park, AP6C
North Chicago, IL 60064

Andrus Foundation
1909 K. Street, N.W.
Washington, D.C. 20049

Atlantic Richfield Foundation
515 South Flower Street
Los Angeles, CA 90071

Beverly Foundation
841 S. Fair Oaks
Pasadena, CA 91105

Doheny Foundation
714 West Olympic Blvd., Rm. 510
Los Angeles, CA 90015

Dreyfus Foundation
575 Madison Avenue
New York, NY 10022

Hartford Insurance Group Foundation
Hartford Plaza
Hartford, CT 06115

Hospital Corporation of America Foundation
One Park Plaza
Nashville, TN 37203

Irvine Foundation
111 Sutter St., Suite 1520
San Francisco, CA 94104

Johnson Foundation
P.O. Box 2316
Princeton, NJ 08540

Kroc Foundation
P.O. Box 547
Santa Ynez, CA 93460

Pfizer Foundation
235 E. 42nd Street
New York, NY 10017

Prudential Foundation
15 Prudential Plaza
Newark, NJ 07101

Retirement Research Foundation
325 Touhy Avenue
Park Ridge, IL 60068

Warner-Lambert Foundation
201 Tabor Rd.
Morris Plains, NJ 07950

VI. SOURCES OF MEDICAL INFORMATION AND ASSISTANCE

The American Medical Association Family Medical Guide,
Editor-in-Chief: Jeffrey R.M. Kunz, M.D.
Random House, New York, 1982

The Consumer's Book of Health: How to Stretch Your Health Care Dollar, by Jordan Braverman
The Saunders Press, Philadelphia, 1982

Good Housekeeping Family Guide to Medications, rev. ed., by Judith K. Jones
Hearst Books, New York, 1980

The New York Times Guide to Personal Health,
by Jane E. Brody
Avon books, New York, 1983

The Physician's Desk Reference
Publisher, Jack E. Angel, 37th edition
Medical Economics Co., Inc., 1983
Oradell, New Jersey

VII. NATIONAL ORGANIZATIONS

The following national organizations provide information resources. Many of these organizations have a variety of publications, including newsletters, available. Many will give information on local activities; some offer workshops. When you write to one of these organizations, always be specific about what you want and how you plan to use the information. This will make it easier for the organization to help you. Check your telephone directory for local branches.

BONE AND JOINT DISEASES

American Academy of Orthopaedic Surgeons (AAOS)
444 N. Michigan Avenue
Chicago, IL 60611
Founded 1933

Arthritis Foundation (Rheumatic Diseases) (AF)
3400 Peachtree Road, N.E.
Atlanta, GA 30326
Founded 1948

National Institute of Arthritis, Metabolism and Digestive Diseases (NIAMDD)
Westwood Building, Room 637
Bethesda, MD 20205
Founded 1950

The Paget's Disease Foundation, Inc.
325 Engle Street
Tenafly, NJ 07670
Founded 1978

BRAIN DISORDERS

Alzheimer's Disease and Related Disorders Assn., Inc. (ADRDA)
360 North Michigan Avenue, Suite 601
Chicago, IL 60601
Founded 1979

Association for Retarded Citizens (Mental Retardation) (ARC)
2501 Avenue J
Arlington, TX 76011
Founded 1950

CANCER

American Cancer Society (ACS)
777 Third Avenue
New York, NY 10017
Founded 1913

Cancer Connection (CC)
H & R Block Building
4410 Main Street,
Kansas City, MO 64111
(816) 932-8453 HOTLINE
Founded 1980

Cancer Information Service
Sponsored by the Department of Health and Human Services
(Many local centers)
1-800-4-CANCER

DENTAL

American Dental Association (ADA)
211 E. Chicago Avenue
Chicago, IL 60611
Founded 1859

DIABETES
American Diabetes Association (ADA)
2 Park Avenue
New York, NY 10016
Founded 1940

FOOT DISORDERS
American Podiatry Association (APA)
20 Chevy Chase Circle, N.W.
Washington, D.C. 20015
Founded 1912

HEARING DISORDERS
American Speech-Language-Hearing Association (ASLHA)
10801 Rockville Pike
Rockville, MD 20852
Founded 1925

National Association of the Deaf (NAD)
814 Thayer Avenue
Silver Spring, MD 20910
Founded 1880

HEART PROBLEMS
American Heart Association
7320 Greenville Avenue
Dallas, TX 75231
Founded 1924

HOSPICES
National Hospice Organization (NHO)
1909 N. Fort Myer Drive, Suite 402
Arlington, VA 22209
Founded 1977

HOSPITAL ACCREDITATION
Joint Commission on Hospital Accreditation (JCAH)
875 N. Michigan Avenue
Chicago, IL 60611

LUNG DISORDERS
American Lung Association (ALA)
1740 Broadway
New York, NY 10019
Founded 1904

Emphysema Anonymous, Inc. (EAI)
Box 66
Fort Myers, FL 33902
Founded 1965

MEDICINE
American Medical Association (AMA)
535 Dearborn Street
Chicago, IL 60610
Founded 1847

NERVOUS SYSTEM DISORDERS

American Academy of Neurology
4015 W. 65th Street, Suite 302
Minneapolis, MN 55435
Founded 1948

National ALS Foundation (Neurological Disorders and Lou Gehrig Disease) (NALSF)
185 Madison Avenue
New York, NY 10016
Founded 1971

National Multiple Sclerosis Society (NMSS)
205 E. 42nd Street
New York, NY 10016
Founded 1946

National Parkinson Foundation (NPF)
1501 N.W. Ninth Avenue
Miami, FL 33136
Founded 1957

Parkinson's Disease Foundation (PDF)
William Black Medical Research Building
Columbia Presbyterian Medical Center
640 W. 168th Street
New York, NY 10032
Founded 1959

United Parkinson Foundation (UPF)
220 S. State Street
Chicago, IL 60604
Founded 1963

NURSING

American Nurses' Association (ANA)
2420 Pershing Road
Kansas City, MO 64108
Founded 1896

PHARMACEUTICALS

Pharmaceutical Manufacturers Association (PMA)
1100 15th Street, N.W.
Washington, D.C. 20005
Founded 1958

Proprietary Association (PA)
1700 Pennsylvania Avenue, N.W.
Washington, D.C. 20006
Founded 1881

PHARMACY

American Pharmaceutical Assoc. (APhA)
2215 Constitution Ave, N.W.
Washington, D.C. 20037
Founded 1852

PSYCHIATRIC-PSYCHOLOGICAL DISORDERS

American Psychiatric Association (Psychiatry) (APA)
1700 18th Street, N.W.
Washington, D.C. 20009
Founded 1844

American Psychological Association (Psychiatry) (APA)
1200 17th Street, N.W.
Washington, D.C. 20036
Founded 1892

SELF-CARE AND SELF-HELP

Children of Aging Parents (CAPS)
2761 Trenton Avenue
Levittown, PA 19056
Founded 1977

The National Self-Help Clearinghouse (NSHC)
33 W. 42nd Street, Rm 1227
New York, NY 10036
Founded 1976

The Self-Help Center (SHC)
1600 Dodge Avenue
Evanston, IL 60204
Founded 1974

SRx Regional Program (Medication Education for Seniors)
1182 Market Street, Room 204
San Francisco, CA 94102
Founded 1977

SKIN DISORDERS

American Academy of Dermatology (AAD)
820 Davis Street
Evanston, IL 60201
Founded 1938

American Dermatological Association (ADA)
Medical College of Georgia
Augusta, GA 30912
Founded 1876

Dermatology Foundation (DF)
820 Davis Street
Evanston, IL 60201
Founded 1967

SPEECH DISORDERS

American Speech-Language-Hearing Association (ASHA)
10801 Rockville Pike
Rockville, MD 20852
Founded 1925

VETERANS

U.S. Veterans Administration
810 Vermont Ave, N.W.
Washington, D.C. 20420

Veterans Administration
Consumer Information Center
Department N
Pueblo, CO 81009

Veterans Benefits for Older Americans
Office of Public and Consumer Affairs, MS061
810 Vermont Ave, N.W.
Washington, D.C. 20420

VISION PROBLEMS

American Association of Opthalmology (AAO)
1100 17th Street, N.W.
Washington, D.C. 20036
Founded 1956

American Federation of Catholic Workers for the Blind and Visually Handicapped (AFCWBVH)
c/o Xavier Society for the Blind
154 E. 23rd Street
New York, NY 10010
Founded 1954

American Foundation for the Blind (AFB)
15 West 16th Street
New York, NY 10011
Founded 1921

Blind Services Association (BSA)
127 N. Dearborn Street, Room 1628
Chicago, IL 60602
Founded 1924

Braille Institute (Blind) (BI)
741 N. Vermont Avenue
Los Angeles, CA 90029
Founded 1918

Christian Record Braille Foundation (Blind) (CRBF)
4444 S. 52nd Street
Lincoln, NE 68506
Founded 1899

Jewish Braille Institute of America (Blind) (JBIA)
110 East 30th Street
New York, NY 10016
Founded 1931

National Library Service
Library of Congress
Washington, D.C. 20542
Founded 1931
(provides library services for blind and physically disabled persons)

RP Foundation Fighting Blindness (Retinitis Pigmentosa)
National Headquarters
1401 Mt. Royal Avenue, 4th Floor
Baltimore, MD 21217

VIII. *Organizations of Geriatric Professionals*

American Association of Geriatric Psychiatric (AAGP)
230 N. Michigan Avenue, Suite 2400
Chicago, IL 60601
Founded 1978

American Geriatrics Society (AGS)
Ten Columbus Circle
New York, NY 10019
Founded 1942

American Society on Aging (ASA)
833 Market Street, Suite 516
San Francisco, CA 94103
Founded 1954

Gerontological Society of America (GSOA)
1835 K Street, N.W., Suite 305
Washington, D.C. 20006
Founded 1945

Appendix B

MEDICAL TERMS COMMONLY USED IN NURSING HOMES

The following terms, which are frequently used—and often abbreviated—in nursing homes, are defined here to help you understand the terminology you will be reading in the resident's medical records. The definitions are not intended to provide medical advice for individual problems. For particular problems, advice and treatment, the reader should consult a physician.

ABRASION: An abrasion results from scraping the skin.

ACUTE (illness): One with rapid onset, severe symptoms and a short course.

A.D.L.: Activities of daily living.

AMBULATORY: Able to walk about.

AMBULATORY WITH ASSISTANCE: Able to walk with the aid of a cane, crutch, brace, wheelchair, walker or another person. Here is an example of charting in the nurses' notes:

"Pt. amb. c cane c assist" means that the patient is ambulatory with a cane and with the assistance of an aide.

ANGINA PECTORIS: Severe pain in the region of the heart, radiating to the left shoulder and, many times, down the left arm.

APHASIA: Loss or impairment of the power to use words, usually resulting from a brain lesion.

B&B: Bowel and bladder: organs of elimination (bowel, bladder, urinary tract). A bowel and bladder program is a plan for relearning the use of the organs of elimination.

B.P.: Blood pressure.

CARDIAC: Pertaining to the heart; a person suffering from a heart condition.

CEREBRAL: Pertaining to the brain.

CHRONIC (illness): One that is long and drawn out; not acute.

CHUX: Trade name for a disposable pad that is soft and absorbent on one side and waterproof on the other; used under incontinent persons or under draining areas of the body. Ambeze, Attends, Dundee, Depend, Ultigards, Geri-Care, Dripride and Convatec are other trade names.

COMA: A state of unconsciousness from which one cannot be roused.

C.V.A.: Cerebral vascular accident. A stroke; causes include blood clot, hemorrhage, compression, spasm.

CYANOSIS: Bluish color to skin due to lack of oxygen.

DEHYDRATION: Lack of adequate fluid in the body; a crucial factor in the health of older people.

DIET, MODIFIED: Nutrient content is changed, caloric content controlled, or consistency altered.

DIET, STRICTLY CONTROLLED: Requires exact calculations, such as caloric or salt content, or purchase of special foods. Intake and output are monitored.

DISORIENTED: Loss of bearing with respect to time, place or identity. Partially refers to disorientation in one or two areas only. Intermittent or occasional disorientation refers to alternating periods of awareness and unawareness.

EDEMA: Swelling of a body part due to the presence of fluid in the tissue.

EMBOLISM: Obstruction of a blood vessel by foreign substance or a blood clot.

FLEXION: Ability to bend.

FR: Fraction.

GERICHAIR: A wheelchair that cannot be self-propelled.

HEMATOMA: A tumor or swelling containing blood; a "black and blue mark."

HYPERTENSION: High blood pressure.

METASTASIS: Movement of bacteria or disease from one part of the body to another.

POSEY BELT (TRADE NAME): Commonly called restraints. Used to secure resident in various positions, such as in a wheelchair, in order to ensure safety and well-being. It must be issued by a doctor's order, or there is a possibility of a lawsuit for illegal restraint.

PRN ("Pro re nata"): An abbreviation used to indicate that a medication is given or treatment performed only as the need arises—in short, as necessary.

PRESSURE SORES/PRESSURE ULCERS (Decubiti/Bedsores): Tissue breakdown causing ulceration of the skin and soft tissue.

R.O.M.: Range of motion; the extent of motion within a given joint.
ACTIVE ROM: Motion carried out voluntarily by the patient.
ACTIVE-ASSISTIVE ROM: Motion carried out voluntarily by the patient with some assistance.
PASSIVE ROM: Motion is initiated and carried through entirely by someone other than the patient.

R.O.: Reality orientation: R.O. is a continuous twenty-four-hour process through which those patients who are disoriented or who have moderate or severe brain damage are encouraged to compensate for lost mental capabilities and to strengthen those that still exist. Others, who are slightly confused, perhaps because of cerebral arteriosclerosis, hearing or vision problems, also can benefit from R.O.

RESTRAINTS: Devices used to restrict activity or to keep patients in one position or area when they would otherwise require frequent checking to ensure safety. Posey belts, leg restraints, wrist restraints, paddle mittens, half doors, and gerichairs are all restraints.

TPR: Temperature, pulse and respiration.

TREMOR: A continuous quivering or shaking motion of a part of the body.

TURN Q2H: Turn every two hours. (A resident who is unable to move herself or himself for a physical or mental reason must be turned frequently to a different position.)

UNRESPONSIVE: Unconscious, semiconscious, stuperous or unusually lethargic.

VITAL SIGNS: Temperature, pulse, respiration and blood pressure.

WALKER: A lightweight frame a person holds in front of himself or herself to give stability in walking. It offers more stability than a cane.

Appendix C

LEGAL ISSUES OF SPECIAL CONCERN TO NURSING HOME RESIDENTS AND THEIR FAMILIES

This appendix is designed to help you and your relative or friend better understand some of the legal terminology and problems you might come across during your involvement with a nursing home. On several occasions you may need the advice and help of a lawyer to examine the admissions contract, to update wills, to assist with the sale of the resident's home and so on.

You may be tempted to try to solve some of these without expert legal advice, but in certain situations you will be well advised to consult an attorney. If you do not have an attorney, a way to locate one is to consult the latest edition of the *Martindale-Hubbell Legal Directory* (a set of volumes found in most libraries that lists lawyers by city and state) or to contact the local bar association. You might also ask friends who have had similar problems to recommend an attorney. Quite often the local senior center can be of help. Before finally selecting an attorney, however, ask about fees. For additional information, contact:

American Bar Association
Commission on Legal Problems of the Elderly
1800 M Street, N.W., Suite 200
Washington, D.C. 20036

Legal Counsel for the Elderly (LCE)
Sponsored by AARP
1909 K Street, N.W.
Washington, D.C. 20049

Civil Liability of Nursing Homes

The criteria used to determine a nursing home's liability for injuries sustained by its residents are the same, somewhat imprecise standards applicable to doctors and hospitals. For the purposes of civil liability, a nursing home is considered a health care provider and is held accountable for the same level of skill exercised by other practitioners in the area. To establish a case of liability, the injured party must prove, generally through the testimony of other nursing home operators and other medical professionals, that the treatment of the injured resident did not measure up to the community standard.

Amazingly few civil lawsuits for personal injuries have been filed by residents against nursing homes—compared with the proliferation of medical malpractice actions in recent years against doctors and hospitals. There are a number of reasons for this. First, an injury suffered by a nursing home resident is not "worth" what a younger claimant would receive for the same injury, since the resident will not have any wage loss to show. Also, the award for pain and suffering, even for a permanent orthopedic injury, would be quite modest, as a reflection of a resident's limited life expectancy. In addition, the resident's general health may previously have been so debilitated that it may be difficult to prove in court what portion of the total problem resulted from the home's malpractice and what portion from the preexisting conditions. It is often impossible to establish the conduct of the home's employees, since the resident may be senile or confused as to what happened. If it comes down to the word of an employee against the confused story of the resident, the home will generally prevail—even though there may be abstract sympathy for the injured resident.

Even if it is possible to reconstruct the exact conduct of the home's employees, it is still necessary to prove that such conduct was a departure from the standard of care prevailing in the industry. This, of course, requires that the resident procure another operator to testify against the nursing home, which may be difficult since nursing home operators, like doctors, may be reluctant to criticize a fellow professional unless the home's performance was outrageously bad—in which case (ironically) expert testimony may not be necessary to establish negligence.

Beyond the traditional legal considerations of proving liability and damages, there are usually psychological, humanitarian and economic forces at play that discourage personal injury cases against nursing homes. Sometimes it will appear to a jury that the claimant is being manipulated into bringing the lawsuit by an artful or scheming child who stands to profit, through inheritance, from any judgment awarded. Such a perception will cause any award to be smaller. The resident may still want to remain at the home, and this would naturally discourage a lawsuit that could only create an atmosphere of hostility and the fear of possible retribution. The resident's family may also feel that the risk of a negative health impact from a trial (with courtroom testimony and sometimes vigorous cross-examination) outweighs any possible monetary benefit to be derived from the experience.

The standard retainer agreement (called a contingency fee contract) provides that the attorney's fee will be a percentage of any judgment returned or settlement obtained. If the lawsuit is unsuccessful, the attorney earns no fee. Most attorneys will decline a case with prospects of only a minimal fee in return for a large expenditure of effort and expenses (including the considerable expense of presenting medical doctors to testify in court).

In the past decade there has been a proliferation of statutes in many states responding to the so-called "medical malpractice crisis." The common result of most of these remedial statutes is regulations that limit the percentages allowable under contingency fee contracts in lawsuits brought against health care professionals. You should obviously become familiar with the statutory attorney fee limitations in your own state *before* signing any contingency fee contract.

These comments should not, however, deter an injured resident from seeking legal advice. There will always be cases where the injuries are significant and clearly caused by the incident in question, and where the home's conduct was clearly both the cause of the problem and a negligent departure from the standard of care. Since this may not be apparent to the resident or family, you should consult an attorney. The threat of civil liability is in itself a deterrent to slipshod practice by most local bar associations on a city or county level. An initial free consultation of one-half hour to an hour is fairly common.

Residents' Rights As Tenants

Laws governing the relationship between landlords and tenants have little application to the legal relationships between a nursing home and its residents. That relationship is defined by the contract entered into between the parties at the outset.

The resident's stay at the home is not an unqualified one in perpetuity. The home, for instance, does not remain obligated to maintain a resident who fails to pay the carrying charge and cannot qualify for federal or state subsidies. A resident with acute health care needs will have to be hospitalized, and this is generally spelled out in the contract. The question of hospitalization gives rise to the related question of the right of the resident to reserve a place on return. Because of the shortage of nursing home beds in some states, beds are generally reserved for only a short time in the resident's absence. Policies on this subject may vary with the locality and individual home, and the resident should make a point of discovering this information before taking up residence.

Trusts

Residents of nursing homes may be better able to pay for their stay if they are designated the beneficiary of short-term trusts established by relatives. Such trusts are typically set up by other family members with larger personal incomes than the resident in order to attribute the income from the trust assets to the beneficiary (the nursing home resident) who is in a lower tax bracket. The establishment of a short-term trust benefits both the grantor (by reducing his or her taxable income) and the beneficiary (by defraying the expenses of the home).

The conditions imposed by the Internal Revenue Service for establishing such a trust require rather detailed legal advice tailored to the specific facts of each case. In general, this type of trust must remain in existence for a minimum number of years and the grantor must retain no control over the assets (corpus) that comprise the trust. Trusts of this type are commonly known as Clifford trusts, from the landmark U.S. Supreme Court opinion that initially considered this topic. The complex mechanics of setting up an appropriate trust will require the advice of professionals in the field of tax law.

Wills

The same rules of execution, witnessing and contesting wills apply whether or not the testator (someone who is making a will or who has made a will) is a resident of a nursing home. One practical consideration, however, is that a nursing home resident's will is more likely to be contested by disillusioned or disinherited relatives on the grounds of a testator's lack of mental capacity or improper influence. Ideally, wills should be executed *before* the person enters the home. If this has not been done, care must be taken not only to execute the document properly, but also to have disinterested witnesses who will be able to verify the testator's mental capacity at the time the will is executed.

Wills are essential to ensure that the resident's property descends to the persons of his or her choice. Without a valid will, the entire estate passes by statute to relatives according to degree of kinship with the testator. This may or may not be what the testator wishes. The laws of descent will not reflect the resident's choice and are a poor substitute for a will.

Simple wills can be drawn up without assistance from attorneys. The more assets one has to dispose of, however, the better it is to seek legal consultation. This will ensure not only that all assets are distributed, but also that the various possible contingencies (for example, one beneficiary dying before other beneficiaries) are covered. Regarding the tax implications and relative benefits of wills versus trusts, you should once again consult with an attorney and perhaps an accountant as well.

Health Care Directives

A health care directive is an instruction from a competent individual to his or her family, representative, health care providers and attorney to stop or continue medical care if that individual becomes incompetent. Like all legal documents, a health care directive must be in writing, signed and witnessed in order to ensure, in the event of incompetence, that one's wishes are protected and obeyed. States with natural death laws specify how the document should be executed. In states without such laws, an attorney can draw one up.

Concerning nursing home residents, such a document should be part of his or her permanent record, kept at the home with copies made available for the resident's representative.

Since at this time no uniform laws exist nationwide concerning the issue of the right to live or die, check with your attorney regarding the laws in your state that govern the following directives:

1. Living Will
2. Durable Power of Attorney
3. Directives to Physicians

Index

Federal regulations, *see* Government regulation of nursing homes
Finances, management of, 34, 77–78, 121
 reviewing the bills, 119–20
Financial facts, 8–14, 44–45
 family responsibility, 12–14
 Medicaid, 11–12
 Medicare, 9–10
 private health insurance plans, 11
 see also Costs of care
Fingernails, 109
Fire safety precautions, 53, 68
Flooring, 52
Flowers, 95
Foley catheters, 109
Food:
 at adult day care programs, 26
 at congregate housing, 30
 as gifts, 95, 99
 Meals-on-Wheels, 33
 at nursing homes, 103, 104
  evaluating, 59–60, 70–71, 106
  service of, 60, 71, 106
 at residential care homes, 29
 at senior apartments, 31
 at senior centers, 33
Food and Drug Administration, 5
Foundations concerned with aging, 144–45
Friends:
 distant, keeping in touch with, 100
 visits by, 91, 93
Funeral arrangements, 78

Geriatric medicine, 4, 5
Geriatric screening programs, 5
Gerichair, 83
Gifts:
 for residents, 95–98
 for staff members, 90
Government regulation of nursing homes, 45–47, 58, 78, 128
 "Patients Bill of Rights" and, 120–23
 on plan of care, 110–11
 registering complaints, 127–28
 staffing regulations, 43–44
 see also Inspection of nursing homes; Licensing
Grievance committees, 124
Grooming of residents, 58–59, 106, 109
 personal care items for, 81
Guardian, 123
Guest book, 98
Guilt of adult children, 2, 37
Gynecologist, 109

Hair, cutting and washing of, 58–59
 see also Grooming; Personal care services
Handicapped:
 congregate housing for the, 30–31
 "talking books" for the, 97
 visually, 97
Handmade gifts, 98
Health and Safety Code, Section 1320 of, 122
Health care directives, 162–63
Health department, state, 127
Hearing aids, 83, 94
Hobbies, 91, 96
Holding a bed, 64, 161
Home, remaining at, 16
 alternative living arrangements, 17, 28–33
 in-home and day care services, 16, 17, 19–26
Home health care services, 19, 22–23, 24
Homemaker-chore services, in-home, 20, 23, 24
Horner, Joyce, 89
Hospice care, 27–28
Hospital association, local, 127
Hospital discharge planner, 36, 39
Housekeeping services, 16, 28, 30, 31

Income of older person, 9
Incontinent residents, 58, 80, 99, 108
Independence of older person, 7–8, 20, 31, 78
In-home and day care services, 16, 17, 19–24

INDEX